THE AUTHENTIC GARDEN

RICHARD HARTLAGE | AND | SANDY FISCHER

THE AUTHENTIC
Garden

NATURALISTIC AND CONTEMPORARY

LANDSCAPE DESIGN

THE MONACELLI PRESS

Library of Congress Control Number:
2015938540

Printed in China

10 9 8 7 6 5 4 3 2 1

First edition

Designed by Mark Melnick

www.monacellipress.com

To the generations of gardeners who inspired a passion for the craft in me:

A.J. 'Bud' Hartlage, Marcella Shelburne, and Floyd and Shirley Hartlage

R H

To my family: Larry, Sean, and Dylan, my parents Barb and Fred Otto.

To my teachers, clients, and colleagues who have shared in and supported my

lifelong passion and exploration of landscape as both place and process.

S F

CONTENTS

Introduction

CHAPTER 1

Plants as Architecture

CHAPTER 2

Artfully Naturalistic Gardens

CHAPTER 3

Graphic Planting Design

Hestercombe, in Somerset, England, is exalted as the finest example of the collaborations between Edwin Lutyens and Gertrude Jekyll. It has been fully restored in recent years and is open to the public.

INTRODUCTION

RICHARD HARTLAGE

I start with the premise that very little is new in design, but I still can't help being enthusiastic about so much that I see. Garden designers all stand on the tilled ground of the practitioners that came before us. Great revelations are rare. Design trends are a continuum of ideas connected in new forms; they are the result of incremental shifts that move from one oeuvre to the next with messy overlaps. These overlaps, however, are where distinct ideas become clear in hindsight. Today the easy, free interchange of ideas expedites the creation of both trends and traditions in any given discipline. At times we are left guessing whether a good idea will be just a temporary fad or become imbedded at a deeper level and ultimately be accepted as part of a bigger movement. Now more than in the past, many ideas are proposed and explored concurrently, crossing disciplinary boundaries and combining in more fluid and amorphous ways. In the past, single ideas could start whole movements. Modern communication and information technology is fast and immediate, and therefore proponents of new thinking are recognized faster and their ideas may be either quickly discounted or adopted at record speed. Traveling around the country and photographing gardens for this book allowed me to see the work of many firms firsthand. I noticed a trend: designers who really know plants and who are comfortable using a variety of plants tend to practice multiple design styles. Only a few firms have signature styles and stay within those confines.

I observed that the ideas espoused by the pioneers of modern landscape architecture are shifting. In the United States, Dan Kiley, James Rose, and Garrett Eckbo were the

most influential landscape designers of the last two generations. This triumvirate championed functionality, embracing bold forms, and instituting a simplicity and clarity of spatial frameworks. Complexity and decoration in planting designs were abandoned as the trio embraced modernist architecture, modern building materials, and created gardens that reflected a clarity of purpose. I want to be clear that this is not a criticism; their new approach to the design of outdoor space was an innovative and appropriate reaction to the culture and needs of the era. World War II was over; the G.I. Bill created a vibrant and engaged middle class in need of housing that supported a lifestyle that included leisure time and recreation. Living in a modern world meant a further separation from the agrarian past and a full embrace of industry, mass production, and technology. A five-day workweek could support a family and a suburban lifestyle that included a variety of recreational pursuits on the weekends.

The next generation, the baby boomers, were avid home gardeners. They are now retiring, downsizing, and simplifying their lives. Part of aging means giving up the garden and backaches. The days of the single-income household and spacious yards have also passed. With both members of a couple working, there is simply less time to maintain a garden. There are, interestingly, two influences on garden design coming

ABOVE: Great Dixter, in East Sussex, England, was the home of the late gardener and gardening writer Christopher Lloyd. Its current head gardener, Fergus Garrett, manages the property after Lloyd's original vision—in the romantic English cottage style.

RIGHT: Lloyd's famed mixed border follows the principles espoused by Jekyll and Robinson; the color palette is very saturated, however, and often employs intense contrasts.

Yew hedges frame most individual garden spaces at Great Dixter
and contain the profusion of plants. Here, tropical and temperate
plants are combined to create a varied experience.

At Sissinghurst in Kent, England, Harold Nicolson structured yew and boxwood hedges for his wife, Vita Sackville-West, to infill with the white and green flowers and silver foliage that became justifiably famous and are often imitated to this day. She chose white flowers for this portion of the garden so they and their guests would be able to see them after dark, on their way to dinner in the adjacent cottage.

from different ends of the demographic spectrum. First, the wealthy are building private gardens and estates at a record rate. Second, people are migrating to cities and urbanites and people with average or lower incomes are again valuing public parks and gardens. In response to changes in the culture and values of our times, then, the paradigm for parks and gardens is again changing. Botanical gardens are no longer the only institutions that truly value plants and use them to create extraordinary places. Public places such as the High Line in Manhattan, Millennium Park in Chicago, and Citygarden in St. Louis are excellent examples of interactive landscapes and lush, multiseasonal gardens. These places are free to the public, focus on leisure, and embrace the performing and visual arts. And people throng to them.

Vibrant public gardens embrace great planning and design. We have seen that innovative spaces rich in materials and expressive plantings create successful experiences. Along with this comes the realization that amazing gardens drive economics by engaging those that live nearby, attracting and generating tourism and furthering development. These powerful economic attributes make capital investment in gardens and their ongoing operational costs worthwhile, which more cities are recognizing. The environmental benefits of green spaces are also being embraced in both urban and suburban settings. It is not surprising that the best and most competitive design firms are now either employing people who can manipulate plants in extraordinary ways or are hiring talented plantspeople on a project-by-project basis.

Here I can only highlight a handful of many worthy practitioners who have contributed to a continuous chain of ideas and practices. As I began writing this book, I made two assumptions. Both turned out to be false. First, I thought I would find countless young and amazingly talented men and women the rest of the world had not yet heard about. We found a few. Most designers included here are midcareer professionals who are deeply committed to landscape architecture and garden design. They have high standards and know how to run a business. They can create one superb project after another. They are not one-hit wonders, but have drive and discipline and have recognized the single most important requirement for building an influential firm—they impart their love of design and their knowledge of it to their teams. Second, I thought more firms or practitioners would operate solely within

ABOVE: Karl Foerster lived and gardened at his nursery in Potsdam. He was one of the pioneers of the ecological style of planting, and his garden functioned as the testing ground for his ideas.

BELOW: Foerster kept the garden's layout simple so that plants could be appreciated from up close and accessed easily.

the confines of one design tradition. There are those that are most comfortable practicing in one style, to be sure. The great discovery was that people who love plants and who design most are adaptable and practice different styles based on the parameters of the project. What they have in common is a great passion and commitment to learning and testing. The level of commitment I found to making exceptional gardens and landscapes by practices of all sizes was inspiring to experience firsthand where I visited.

PAYING HOMAGE

Many designers past and present have influenced my own aesthetic and, inevitably, the projects that appear later in these pages. Their gardens either appear here or have directly influenced the work of those that do.

Planting design is generally considered to have come into its own at the height of the Arts and Crafts movement, thanks to proponents William Robinson and Gertrude Jekyll. These two garden designers revolutionized and popularized a romantic and complex use of plants. An interest in nature, an expanding selection of available plants, and a wealthy set of patrons converged to form what is still one of the most recognizable garden-making traditions: the English cottage garden. What is often not recognized or is forgotten is that these schemes, which may appear effortless or rambling, take great study and knowledge to achieve. They were often designed in a complex way that related to the architecture of the house. Manual labor was still inexpensive, which allowed them to be carefully cared for—although the Industrial Revolution would soon have

Karl Foerster used a simple water feature to create habitat for aquatic and marginal, or water-loving, plants.

its impact on the availability of affordable maintenance by luring laborers from estates and farms to factories.

By the end of the Arts and Crafts movement in about 1910, the refrain was unanimous on both sides of the Atlantic: good gardeners were hard to find and they were expensive. Only the wealthiest could afford large and complicated gardens. Beatrix Farrand and Ellen Biddle Shipman both complained in their correspondence to clients

Dutch designer Mien Ruys melded planting designs with simple, modernist hardscape elements and forms; she saw this as a way to help the emerging middle classes of the mid-twentieth century maximize the enjoyment of their gardens.

about a lack of skilled labor and increasing cost. Farrand even wrote a maintenance guide for her client and patron Mildred Barnes Bliss to ensure that Dumbarton Oaks would be properly cared for in the event that the maintenance budget for the garden had to be scaled back. She stated the priorities clearly to ensure that her vision for the garden would remain intact. Farrand had also intended to leave her own beloved garden at Reef Point as a research and education center, but realizing she could not secure funding to ensure that it would be maintained at the highest standards after her death, she dismantled the garden herself and sold the plants to her patrons.

Most of the historic references for planting design used by Americans have been English simply because of our national heritage. The Germans and the Dutch, however, have been hugely influential to a smaller circle of designers. Karl Foerster (1874–1970), a German nurseryman, bred many worthy plants, dozens of which have been imported to North America. *Calamagrostis* x *acutiflora* 'Karl Foerster,' which features prominently in these pages, is by far the most recognizable of his contributions. He followed the ideas of Charles Darwin and bred environmentally durable plants. A poet at heart and a prolific writer, he was an early proponent of creating naturalistic plantings based on specimens from the same ecology to decrease watering, maintenance, and fertilization needs. He was in many ways the father of a planting design trend that is presently sweeping across Europe and North America. He was very interested in and worked with many of the prairie and hardy plants of North America, Asia, and Europe. He trialed plants he selected from his nursery in his own garden in Potsdam, which is still maintained today—and open to the public. He was hugely influential and deserves to be better known in the English-speaking world.

Another heroine of mine is the Dutch-born Mien Ruys (1904–1999). She was the daughter of the founder of Moerheim Nursery, who counted Gertrude Jekyll a friend and arranged for Ruys to spend time in her

ABOVE: Mien Ruys often employed strong geometries to form garden rooms; here, a round room's edge is softened by a perennial border.

LEFT: Salvias at Moerheim Nursery, run by Mien Ruys's family; she created famous model gardens there to test her ideas and inspire others.

A weekend home in Petrópolis, a short distance from Rio de Janiero, designed
by Roberto Burle Marx. Patterned lawns were a hallmark of his work.

RIGHT: Burle Marx's background in the visual arts led him to create highly graphic gardens, which in turn have inspired subsequent generations of garden designers and landscape architects to approach planting design in a graphic way.

BELOW: Orange-flowered gingers complement a tile wall designed and painted by Burle Marx. He used influences from opera, painting, and jewelry-making in his gardens.

youth working in Tunbridge Wells. A well-versed designer with a deep knowledge of plants, she was wildly prolific, eventually designing more than 3,000 private and public gardens. Ruys embraced the emerging modernist aesthetic and was a proponent of strong, geometric forms in planting design. She created model gardens at her father's nursery to inspire those who came to buy plants, a catalog of ideas for her clients, and she gave away plant combinations at the nursery. She combined woody plants to create structure, was a huge proponent of hedges, and was deft at naturalistic planting. An early proponent of grasses and low-maintenance schemes, she influenced many landscape designers in Europe, including Piet Oudolf. Moerheim Nursery is still in business, and her model gardens are still being maintained. They will provide invaluable lessons and inspiration for anyone able to make the pilgrimage.

Plantsman and garden designer Piet Oudolf uses his own garden in Hummelo, in the Netherlands, to develop, test, and demonstrate his ideas on planting design. Here, yew hedges are carved into sinuous waves.

Roberto Burle Marx (1909–1994) was trained in opera and self-taught as a painter. Through the encouragement of Oscar Niemeyer, Burle Marx shifted his focus and talents into landscape design. He spent time in Germany, where he was was influenced by the avant-garde movement. Burle Marx almost single-handedly introduced landscape architecture as a profession in Brazil and South America, profoundly influencing the generations of garden designers and landscape architects who have come after him. He designed the gardens; his brother grew the plants and built the projects. Burle Marx is widely known for his promenades in Copacabana and Ipanema, and at Flamengo Park.

Burle Marx had a deep love of plants and was voracious in his acquisition of them. His mother's farms became his home base, botanical garden, and nursery, where he would trial and supply his projects with the plants he needed. He is well known for explorations into his native country to find plants to use in his work; he also imported plants from Asia, South Africa, and Central America to expand his palette, however. He realized there was no real industry in Brazil to help maintain his projects, so he sought out the most durable plants he could find. His style was highly graphic and sculptural. His bold aesthetic was also highly refined and joyous. Once his work began to be published internationally, many designers made pilgrimages to see his projects and to meet him. Raymond Jungles and James van Sweden have both since brought his influence to North America. Burle Marx was engaging and generous with his time, and he enthusiastically transmitted his love of art, landscape design, and plants to anyone who took the time to visit him. I was fortunate enough to meet him a half a dozen times, and my own work has been influenced by him in important ways as well.

Van Sweden and Wolfgang Oehme founded

Even in Oudolf's former nursery stock beds, topiary forms created a backdrop for the plants that were ultimately to be dug and divided.

Oehme, van Sweden Landscape Architects in 1977. Combining Wolfgang Oehme's training in Germany—and a deep knowledge of plants that harkened back to Karl Foerster's legacy—and Jim's background in architecture, horticulture, and landscape architecture, the two created pioneering work. Their partnership fostered a signature style of durable, temperate plants and a bold, contemporary vision that set landscape architecture on edge when their work first began to be published and seen, and is

Piet Oudolf shaped a yew into an abstract topiary form to create a focal point amid the surrounding mix of perennials in his own garden at Hummelo.

often called the New American Garden. They brought the use of grasses—ironically, often native prairie species that had been exported to Europe—to gardens. The clarity of their vision captured the imagination of public and private clients in the Mid-Atlantic and ultimately throughout temperate America. Jim van Sweden was a friend and while I was managing botanical gardens in the first half of my career, he was seen as one of the most important innovators in the profession.

TOP: Grasses at Hummelo move and catch the evening sun, adding a different type of interest to the garden than blooms alone could supply.

ABOVE: Perennials flowering in late summer in Oudolf's garden, showing the matrix style for which he has since become known.

Oehme, van Sweden's first major public commission was for the Federal Reserve; after its success, many commissions with the government followed. With the subsequent publication of several books—and Jim's social skills—private commissions started rolling in. Although both founders are now sadly departed, the current partners have embraced naturalistic and matrix plantings while allowing for the style to evolve. The Native Plant Garden at the New York Botanical Garden, which opened in 2013, is a masterful example of the firm's superb planting design and thoughtful architectural detailing.

The current emphasis on native plants, however, can cause somewhat of a conundrum. Neil Diebold and his prairie reconstructions came about at the same time as Oehme, van Sweden was developing its aesthetic, and the embrace of prairie plants in their projects has evolved into environmental stewardship. As environmental awareness has grown, the landscape world has changed in radical ways. Plants that were once considered weeds or undesirables have become fashionable. Anyone who has visited the expansive prairie restorations at the Missouri and Chicago Botanical Gardens understands their power. Visitors who experience the short- and tall-grass prairies often come away realizing that many of those plants are the foundations of their own perennial borders, in more refined varieties. The native plant movement is significant for our time, but it is important to note that it is not an option for all applications. In the Pacific Northwest, for example, we have a limited flora that is usable for urban landscape projects; this fact is difficult to impress on potential clients who are already culturally programmed to be particularly sympathetic to environmental concerns. To create extraordinary places with native plants, a rich and complex local flora that is well adapted to a variety of growing conditions and available in the nursery industry is required.

Americans continue look to Europe for fresh ideas as well, however. Piet Oudolf is a notable Dutch plantsman who regularly collaborates with James Corner Field Operations and Gustafson Guthrie Nichol. His most well-known gardens in the United States include the High Line in New York and the Lurie Garden at Millennium Park in Chicago. He is a proponent of perennials, and

While working at historic Wave Hill in the Bronx, Marco Polo Stufano introduced the cottage style of gardening. His background in art history gives him a discerning eye for plant combinations.

of creating gardens that can be appreciated throughout all four seasons by incorporating plants that retain interesting structure even when not in bloom.

Steve Martino, a landscape architect practicing in the Southwest, uses native plants to make current, contemporary gardens that are strikingly architectural. His love of the desert and his keen observation skills have helped him to produce work that is fresh and perhaps more sophisticated than some would expect to be possible using the flora of the region. He is a friend, a mentor, and an inspiration. He keeps his practice small and hands-on so no detail will escape his notice or control. Martino values built materials and details as much as the plants he uses, and this makes his work unique—and a joy to photograph since every view practically frames itself.

A 28-acre gem of a public garden, Wave Hill has been quietly restored and built up by Marco Polo Stufano, a Queens native and son of immigrants from Bari, Italy, since 1967. The site along the banks of the Hudson River just north of Manhattan has influenced many of us who grew up in public gardens. Wave Hill in particular inspires us to embrace the day-to-day joy of the gardening process. Those who can use plants most effectively, in my opinion, are those who still get put hands in the dirt and find pleasure in that connection. The accumulated knowledge it takes to confidently and masterfully design with plants is a commitment that can only be learned by spending hours and days in the garden. The division of labor and the creation of a hierarchy between gardeners, horticulturists, garden designers, and landscape architects is happily starting to erode with the realization that by embracing all these skills amazing, highly valued places can be created and sustained.

LOOKING FORWARD

My reason for writing this book was to acknowledge and celebrate the breadth of talented garden makers and landscape architects practicing in the United States today. Some are single-person practices, but many are small or midsized firms. The work of the larger, established firms is exciting not only because of

In the Wild Garden at Wave Hill, Marco Polo Stufano espoused
William Robinson's tenets, translated for the New York climate.

the final designs, but because the owners/principals are truly committed to teaching their values to their younger employees; their work is as much about creating gardens today as about passing the legacy of the profession on to the next generation.

My goal while employed in public horticulture at the Willowwood and Frelinghuysen Arboretums in North-Central New Jersey and as director of the Elisabeth C. Miller Botanical Garden in Seattle was to educate through comprehensive plant collections. In this context, with the goal of creating and displaying large and complex plant collections, the naturalistic, Arts and Crafts style of planting often worked best. As I have developed a design practice and a wider range of clients and projects, I have come to understand the value of other planting styles, depending upon context. I love the graphic style of planting design for its dramatic and simple clarity of vision. I find it useful, even with perennials and grasses, for forming a strong framework for a project. Once that framework has been fully laid out, I will often take specific blocks and plant them in a matrix or mixed way as contrast to the larger structure—this process of taking pieces of different planting theories and applying them to one project is similar to how trends in the overall profession shift and change gradually as new ideas are introduced.

At Wave Hill, rotating container displays add rich and thoughtful texture in every season.

The professionals who are leading and designing the best projects in the public and private sectors today embrace complexity and depth. Some of the projects that appear here may at first glance appear to be minimalist, but upon closer inspection reveal intriguing nuances. Minimalism is not outdated, but beauty for beauty's sake is making a comeback—it's just that the definition of beauty has evolved. The use of plants to reinforce function, intellectual content, green or ecological strategies, immersive experiences, and, most important, emotion, is in vogue again.

1

Plants AS

ARCHITECTURE

"The energy and space around a material
are as important as the energy and space within."

ANDY GOLDSWORTHY,
A COLLABORATION WITH NATURE

T he interplay between built structures and plants is the very essence of
landscape architecture, and essential to garden- and place-making. All
gardens and landscapes use plants to structure space, but the infinite
ways this can be accomplished are what makes garden design exciting. Trees and
hedges in particular are imperative for dividing, composing, and manipulating
spatial volumes at all scales and sizes.

There is nothing more beautiful than the dappled light and distant view down
an allée, for example, and any existing allée is almost always worth retaining.
Olin Partnership recently took advantage of a double row of London plane trees

LEFT: Topiaries shaped into even simple, clipped forms take years to mature and a skilled gardener to maintain, although depending on conditions and plant species it may only be necessary to trim them once a year.

BELOW: The slight batter to the yew hedge that encloses Longwood's Topiary Garden ensures that the lower branches are not shaded, which helps them retain their density over time.

OPPOSITE: Stacked plates on a topiary are a study in light and shadow; the complexity of the shape was also clearly intended to impress visitors to Longwood, and it succeeds. The tree's style contrasts pleasantly with the simpler obelisk and dome shapes nearby, making for a visual treat.

PREVIOUS PAGES: Light plays across sculptural yews clipped into classic, traditionally inspired forms at Longwood Gardens.

in front of the new Barnes Foundation building in Philadelphia, realizing that the scale of the mature trees would be a fitting interface between the museum and the Benjamin Franklin Parkway—and would make for a sublime stroll for residents and visitors. These regal trees create a visually pervious edge and ceiling to the larger landscape that holds the museum campus, as well as link it to the larger urban setting. This type of dialogue, not merely plants for plants' sake, is the ideal.

Hedges are taking on new life as a creative design element; they have had unbelievable difficulty recovering from their established use as the underpinning of neoclassical gardens, where they were used in formal, axial arrangements. Now, with adept design—and diligent use of shears—they are shaped in expressive, innovative, sculptural, and asymmetric ways. They are less expensive than steel, masonry, or wood to install, and completely plastic in form. In a small urban garden they can become curved walls that expand and contract the volumes of negative space. Ron Lutsko used the interplay between metal, water, and living plant material in a way that is both serene and visually fresh for a small terrace garden in San Francisco. There, organic but tightly composed, cloud-formed boxwoods are a dynamic frame for city views and a good foil for the fleeting seasonality of a few carefully selected varieties of flowers.

Skill is required to envision what is possible and a designer and gardener must be in sync to reach the intended effect, but the results of a willing collaboration are usually compelling.

EARLY PRACTITIONERS

English garden designer Lancelot "Capability" Brown, (1716–1783) and his less-known predecessor William Kent (1685–1748) were two of the first to structure space informally at large scales by using plants. Brown was responsible for the design of many country houses and estates, and he worked with the landed gentry to achieve a look that appeared to be natural or unplanned—though of course it was carefully designed. He reacted against the French and Dutch style of garden-making, which was often patterned or rigidly geometric, and in fact he became known as "the destroyer of formal gardens" for uprooting so many older estate gardens. His work celebrated a Romantic ideal of the agrarian landscape and has become synonymous with what the quintessential eighteenth-century English landscape ought to have looked like. Brown conceived picturesque parks with incredible, long views. His landscapes also manipulated rolling topography, and he occasionally dammed streams to make lakes. He only used trees native to Britain: lots of English oaks, European lindens (*Tilia*), hedge maples, and a very few others. Tree masses were necessarily his primary tool for structuring space and framing views, given the large expanses of the estates at hand. His compositions represent plants as architecture at their most straightforward: on a landscape scale. His influence can still be seen at Blenheim Palace in Oxfordshire and Chatsworth House in Derbyshire, among many other places.

The mottled trunks on a mature allée of London plane trees are a striking complement to the fossilized Israeli limestone that clads the new Barnes Foundation in Philadelphia. *Platanus* x *acerifolia* is used extensively in urban settings across Europe and in the temperate Northeastern United States for its tough constitution and longevity.

Purple-leaved Japanese maples and a wall picturesquely covered with
Boston ivy greet visitors at the entrance to the Barnes Foundation as
they stroll on a path that transects the water feature.

ABOVE: Red-stemmed dogwoods are clipped into a hedge that forms a neat backdrop for a bench. They add interest in winter as well, when the stems turn crimson.

LEFT: European chestnuts have been planted extensively on the Barnes Foundation campus. This tree was widely planted at the turn of the last century, then fell inexplicably out of favor. Together with the autumn hues of the *Itea*, sedges, and shade trees, they create a billowing foundation planting for the building.

ABOVE: Steve Martino plants palo verde trees extensively in his Southwestern gardens; their small leaves, twiggy branch structure, and horizontal growth habit create a dappled shade that gives relief from the strong sun. They are underplanted with golden barrel cactus and agave, which supply a variety of forms, colors, and textures.

LEFT: *Parkinsonia microphylla* and an *Agave sisalana* stand sentinel along the entry walk to a Phoenix garden by Steve Martino.

Humphry Repton (1752–1818), was the last great English landscape designer of the eighteenth century. He is viewed as the successor to Brown, but his style is more eclectic; it retains distant picturesque vistas and reintroduces the formal garden within the domain of the house. His famous Red Books were his "client deliverable." These red, leather-bound books were created for each prospective job and show landscape perspectives with clever pullout tabs and overlays that would indicate suggested improvements in before-and-after iterations. Serious garden designers and avid amateurs should make an effort to see these books. With planning and an appointment, some are available for viewing at the Huntington Library in San Marino, California; the library at the New York Botanical Garden has reprints in its reference collection as

well. Many designers still follow his dictate for designing gardens: place complex architectural, finely detailed, and visually complicated areas near a residence, then let them give way to naturalized and informal spaces as one moves out into the surrounding land.

Ellen Biddle Shipman (1869–1950) adapted her knowledge of the plant palette she used in the Northeast and Midwest to her most important commission, Longue Vue Gardens in New Orleans. Shipman used boxwood extensively and often created spaces that were based on squares and rectangles, such as low hedge frames that spill over with annuals, perennials, and summer-flowering shrubs. She was known for her adept skill at creating romantic flower gardens within a strict architectural frame. Stan Hywet Hall in Akron, Ohio, and Reeves-Reed Arboretum in Summit, New Jersey, are two other examples of her work, have been restored, and are open to the public.

In the modern era, Dan Kiley (1912–2004) used bosques of trees, hedges, and strong architectural forms on the ground plane in a way that was greatly influenced by his travels in Europe and his study of André Le Nôtre (1613–1700), and especially

ABOVE: Steve Martino highlights bougainvillea and ocotillo (*Fouquieria splendens*) as specimens on the edge of a dining terrace. The bougainvillea is pruned heavily to expose its trunk and stems, and is espaliered on a rock wall. Denser plantings would have detracted from the space's austere architecture.

RIGHT: The foliage of *Agave weberi* and a desert ironwood (*Olneya tesota*) benefits from a backdrop of a vibrant orange-red wall, which allows the eye to perceive their forms in detail.

Vaux le Vicomte. His highly structured landscapes featured detailed spaces that were often formal and asymmetrical, with visual connections or borrowed views to the larger vista. Kiley's most famous residential project is the Miller Garden in Columbus, Indiana, which is based on a grid and very rectilinear and architectonic in form; allées radiate from the main residence to create views along axes that lead the eye into the distance. Kiley did not always use straight lines, however, but as a man of his day, explored bold circular and curvilinear forms as well. He often worked with the architect Eero Saarinen (1910–1961), their most famous collaboration being the Jefferson National Expansion Memorial in St. Louis, Missouri, and the landscape surrounding it. There, Kiley designed great circular or looping walks with lines of trees that complemented the Gateway Arch itself.

Today, we can see how another form important in historic European and American gardens—the topiary—must have looked by visiting Longwood Gardens in southeastern Pennsylvania. The extensive display of over fifty forms highlights how topiaries can be both architectural building blocks as well as purely decorative sculptures. Topiaries were counterpoints to nature for seventeenth-century garden

ABOVE: What appears to be a simple *Dasylirion* planted in gravel is, upon closer inspection, a masterful design move by Steve Martino: its dome shape picks up the curve of the low wall, the angle of the sunlight that strikes that portion of the garden illuminates each individual leaf in sharp detail, and a hybrid mesquite tree provides an area of deep shade by way of contrast.

RIGHT: A dense planting of palo verde trees, ocotillos, and various other desert plants screen the house from the street and create a lush vista for anyone sitting on its main terraces.

LEFT: Plants, hardscape elements, art, and furnishings combine in a garden by Steve Martino to offer a dynamic respite from harsh desert and urban surroundings. Ocotillo and variegated agave in particular balance the scale of a sculpture by Fletcher Benton and give dimension and a perimeter to the outdoor "room."

RIGHT: Plants native to Arizona—ocotillo, variegated agave, *Opuntia engelmannii*, and saguaro—are combined in an arrangement that is a distillation of what Mother Nature might have envisioned, which plays their unique forms and textures off each other. The shape of the saguaro's trunk also complements a nearby stoneware sculpture by Jun Kaneko.

The circular pads of the *Opuntia macrocenta* 'Violacea' complement the rounded forms of a metal sculpture by Fletcher Benton in a garden by Steve Martino; both serve as a counterpoint to the rectangular lines of the architecture and terrace. Brittlebush (*Encelia farinosa*) lines the top of the wall, mediating the transition from the garden plantings to the natural landscape beyond.

designers such as Le Nôtre: they imposed a rational form on a living plant, by extension proclaiming man's supremacy over nature. The Topiary Lawn at Great Dixter in Rye, England, provides a slightly more modern and casual take on the form.

Trees and shrubs are critical components in any executed project, partly because they are simply the largest and most permanent elements of any garden. They are also the framework that supports a design's more decorative elements, year round. They serve as living extensions of built architectural elements such as walls, arbors, and fences.

CONTEMPORARY INTERPRETATIONS

Each project featured here responds to historical precedents in some way, but also looks toward the future and brings a unique perspective or interpretation of classic forms. These images illustrate ideas regarding the progression and structuring of space and views, and the practitioners featured have mastered using plants in architectural ways.

Credit is due to Jacques Wirtz and his design firm, Wirtz International Landscape Architects, who are based in Belgium but practice internationally. They are known for shaping and shearing plants—particularly hedges and shrubs—into sculptural and often cloud-like forms that introduce a strong sense of movement. They are also adept with their use of perennials, but this is less known and more rarely photographed because they are more recognized for their bold, architectural treatment of spaces. Wirtz's own garden in Belgium is open to the public, the firm redesigned the Carrousel Garden at the Tuileries in Paris, and soon they will have a commercial project in Midtown Manhattan. Their contribution to contemporary design practice cannot be overstated.

Olin is a landscape architecture, planning, and urban design firm located in Philadelphia. They designed the outdoor spaces for the new Barnes Foundation museum, also located in Philadelphia. The public landscape

BELOW: At dusk, a fire pit and low lights allow the Japanese pine to be appreciated in a different way. The tree is well suited to placement in a Northwest garden since it reinforces Seattle's position on the Pacific Rim.

LEFT: A Japanese black pine trimmed into neat tiers relates to the house's wall of strongly linear windows, as well as bestows an Asian mood to a garden by Randy Allworth on Lake Washington, in Seattle.

ABOVE: In the same garden, another Japanese black pine is used as a Zen-like focal point near the house's front entry. The granite bench and wood siding emphasize the tree's horizontal branches; all the components converge to create a well-thought-out and harmonious space.

ABOVE: Randy Allworth placed four crepe myrtles in a configuration to suggest an outdoor room on a small terrace in Seattle; although they rarely flower in that mild climate, their vase-shaped growth habit, cinnamon-colored bark, and vibrant autumn oranges and reds make them valuable in all seasons.

LEFT: *Sarcococca hookeriana* var. *humilis* is hardy to zone 6 and grows in to make a mid-height ground cover of about twelve inches. Here it is used to create a leafy foreground to a minimalist stone wall in a shady part of a garden; it also perfumes the space starting in late February.

ABOVE: A restrained plant palette of liriope, boxwood, and Portuguese laurel creates a garden of broad geometric gestures by Randy Allworth that supports modern hardscape elements including a tall, minimalist fireplace. A more elaborate planting scheme would have diminished the impact of the site's careful grading.

LEFT: Scotch moss (*Sagina subulata*) planted in a rectangular swath will grow in as an alternative to a grass lawn. It is surrounded with neatly trimmed spheres of boxwood and tufts of deer fern (*Blechnum spicant*), which is native to the Northwest. The matrix plantings of these three in neat formations adds an architectural feel to the overall space.

is asymmetrical, contemporary, and formal—serving as a complementary foreground to the architecture by Tod Williams and Billie Tsien. The landscape connects the site with the fabric of the city and sets the modern building into a series of modern garden spaces that become more detailed and intimate the farther one moves into the site. The interplay between a sculptural water feature, concrete site walls, planters, stone terraces, and ground planes of various stone is rich and complex. All is capped by a majestic allée of plane trees that lies adjacent to the water feature. The trees are bold enough to relate the site to the larger urban context, but their rhythmic trunks also draw the visitor deeper into the site. Shrubs and vines are used in simple but effective ways, mainly at the entrance to soften concrete walls that create courtyards on the interior and as foundation plantings, where low-profile specimens tie the building to the ground and create a human-scaled experience for vistors. A wide selection of deciduous trees as well as coniferous and broad-leaved trees and shrubs create texture and add depth to the landscape. The simple use of 30-foot-high deodar cedars on the south side of the building illustrates how judicious plantings can call attention to architecture's scale.

Steve Martino is a landscape architect from Phoenix. His gardens are very innovative in the way he uses plants as architecture. His use of desert flora and woody lilies—yuccas, agaves, *Nolina*, and *Dasylirion*—is unique in the way they are incorporated to be responsive to the larger environment. His gardens are like theatrical sets: he knows when to use an architectural plant against a plane of colored concrete to highlight it as sculpture for

OPPOSITE, ABOVE: A hedge of cherry laurel, *Prunus caroliniana* 'Monus,' trimmed into a strong, neat line partitions a garden by Ron Lutsko into two rooms. The metal frame that holds it acts as a guide to keep the hedge in proportion. The green joints in the asymmetric pavers are planted with *Thymus serpyllum* 'Minus,' and repeat the strict linearity of the hedge on the ground plane.

OPPOSITE, BELOW: The garden's most rigid material—steel—surprisingly provides its most curvaceous detail; the plants, by contrast, are the space's most architectural element. Even the Sonoma dove tree at left is kept neatly to one side.

LEFT: The walkway through the hedge that joins the two halves of the garden reveals the tension designer Ron Lutsko created between the living and static design elements; the water feature mediates it by adding movement.

BELOW: Horizontal lines contributed by paver joints and built-in trellis bars for an espaliered Meyer lemon tree create a calming visual motif. The silver-leaved bush *Calocephalus brownii* adds a focal point amid the dark green of the other plants.

the most impact, or a mass of softer plants as a wild and wooly background to a seating area. He conceives of each space as a series of views and vignettes that unfold, and works to make them both visually "complete" and striking. He balances complex and simple elements as counterpoints, one to the other. His deep understanding of the native landscape and his strong sense of composition have influenced the last three generations of landscape architects and garden designers in the Southwest. Martino uses fewer cactus than expected, considering the native Arizona landscape, but does introduce them as accents or dramatic focal points. He uses many trees, palo verde being the most common. He also uses herbaceous plants to create a rich fabric that clothes a basic framework of structural plants and built architectural elements.

Martino's work is also nuanced—he has set a series of stove-pipe cactus in silhouette against a glass wall to be backlit by the setting sun, for example. Each plant in his garden is used with considered deliberation, which creates a minimalist feel. A blue-leaved dasylirion simply outlined against a vibrant stone wall may supply the most poignant impression of one of his designs.

Modern aesthetics are often interpreted for gardens as trees and shrubs used in strongly architectural ways. Randy Allworth, in Seattle, and Ron Lutsko, in San Francisco, both emphasize highly disciplined plant forms. In their work, plants are treated more as structural materials than as visual embellishments—they use the living components of a site as direct extensions of its built forms.

LEFT AND ABOVE: Coconut palms, striking against the sky, have a strong connotation with the tropics. Here they frame a pool house—and repeat its architectural detailing. For the dining area of the same property, Nievera Williams added carpentaria palms, a silver bismarckia, at left, and an areca palm, at right, to create a space that feels secluded and lush.

A cheerful and remarkable dome-shaped *Ficus nitida* is perfectly pruned and flanked by a short allée of palms covered with sleeves of confederate jasmine. Diagonal green joints between the pavers add further interest to the ground plane of this highly geometric and formal entryway by Nievera Williams.

Podocarpus macrophyllus is native to southern Japan and hardy to zone 8. Here
it is tightly clipped by Nievera Williams into a niche complete with a layered pool
and an urn that functions as the terminus of the view from an adjoining terrace.

Designer Jack deLashmet created a fanciful, undulating caterpillar of Japanese holly, *Ilex crenata*, to separate the lawn from a cottage's flower garden, behind it. The patterns of sun and shadow on it and the adjacent expanse of grass accentuate its unexpected form.

Alliums in royal purple and white float jauntily as spring turns
to summer in a flower garden that forms a traditional counterpoint to the contemporary form of the holly hedge.

Mario Nievera and Kevin Williams, whose landscape architecture practice Nievera Williams is located in Palm Beach, most often work with traditional aesthetics to create formal gardens with a contemporary mood. Their compositions are notable for their balance of light, form, color, and texture. They are particularly adept at—and admired for—their use of tropical and subtropical flora, and they are masters of selecting plants that succeed at conveying a sense of geometry and architecture even in the humid Floridian climate, which represents a deep understanding of their material.

The work of Doyle Herman Design Associates and Jack deLashmet may differ aesthetically, but both are proponents of using green hedges as architectural statements. Doyle Herman tends to rely on European and formal design references in its projects, while deLashmet often references more organic forms. Their work shows how values are shifting—there was a perception for the better part of the last century that clipping hedges was a waste of time, costly, and burdensome to the owner. Recently however, the focus on green building and the environmental benefits of plants, coupled with low cost of installation, have helped hedges make a resurgence. There is no better tall hedge than *Carpinus betulus*, and the reappearance of it in the nursery industry is a direct response to an increase in demand; it used to be nearly impossible to find or, if found, the plants were often limbed up six to eight feet, precluding use as a hedge. Growers on both coasts are now producing low-branched trees for specific use as a clipped hedge.

OPPOSITE: Repetition in a garden can be restful to the eye. Doyle Herman uses familiar plants such as yew, boxwood, and hornbeams in strictly clipped, geometric forms to create prescribed sight lines and pathways with intuitive circulation patterns.

ABOVE: Boxwood hedges are a mainstay of space-making on large and small scales. When creatively and logically designed, however, they continue to engage. Here pleached hornbeams and conical shrubs provide a background to boxwood squares filled with additional hornbeams to create a subtle study in greens.

Boxwoods have always been, and will remain, a mainstay. Like hornbeams, boxwoods take pruning, shearing, pinching, and clipping very well. They can also be grown as specimens and are the most pliable of any plant for manipulating into rectilinear or sculptural forms. Hollies and camellias are other appropriate options for architectural hedges in temperate climates, and a survey of recent work reveals that they are currently being used as such extensively throughout Asia, Europe, and North America.

USING ARCHITECTURAL ELEMENTS

Designers who allow plants to drive a garden's scheme usually conceive of the landscape in a series of layers. Although this seems obvious, it isn't always understood. Many firms think about the design process and approach documentation of the

Buttresses of hornbeam (*Carpinus betulus*) harken back to Edwardian gardens.
Doyle Herman uses them to romantic effect, framing a long vista that terminates
at a bench in the distance. Their intriguing form helps to separate and highlight
the perennials, which make a patrician statement in this arrangement.

Three trees—a Korean dogwood, a weeping beech, and a tupelo—have enough contrast in form to be seen as individuals even as Doyle Herman has them work together to create a perimeter for an expanse of lawn. The architecture of the mature trees, coupled with a moody sky, create a memorable sense of place.

A staccato effect created by a row of pyramidal yews, *Taxus cuspidata* 'Capitata' is balanced by a lower, looser arrangement of boxwood-enclosed herbs in a garden by Doyle Herman.

European copper beeches are an expressive feature in an estate-scaled landscape by Doyle Herman. Their foliage leads the eye through their formal
lanes out and to the autumn trees beyond, even as their tightly clipped forms
contrast with shapes of the trees' natural canopies.

construction drawings in exactly this way. Trees and large-scale shrubs are considered first, to form and shape the overall spaces. Smaller woody plants and perennials are added to create another layer and develop interest on the ground plane. Last, bulbs and annuals are introduced for seasonal color and interest—although landscape designers often do not create a planting plan for bulbs and annuals. For these more ephemeral plants, it often suffices to create a spreadsheet with a list of names and the general quantities desired, then to place them by sight in the field after the rest of a project is installed.

Styles vary, yet the structuring of space—whether formal or more informal—is a basic tenet of successful garden- and place-making. So many plant lovers and home gardeners overlook the importance of first defining space with large-scale plants to create an outline for a garden before filling it with "botanical flourishes." The single biggest mistake the amateur gardener makes is filling the land with a large variety of plants with no regard for organizing space. What is an herbaceous planting without a wall to display it against, for example? This is a classic way to approach making a green space, but it results in a plant collection and not a garden. It may be lovely to walk through, but if there is no shady place to sit and enjoy the garden, all the paths are the same size so there is no intuitive circulation plan, and, most important, there are no large-scale plants to indicate to the visitor where to look in the garden or where the end destination is, it unsettles us on a subconscious level. To create a space with a sense of place and to make a memorable experience, plants with character and structure must provide various visual guideposts at intervals throughout a garden. Trees and shrubs, as the living "skeleton" of any landscape, are essential—they can even be the whole story when done well. The rest of this book references them as critical elements in any successful garden.

Beech in two incarnations are juxtaposed for maximum impact. A specimen-sized European copper beech is planted here in juxtaposition with a hedge of the same plant by Doyle Herman. The hedge's bold curves are a strong and pleasantly unexpected design move for the pastoral setting. Beech hedges must be started small so the trees can be planted closely—usually two feet on center—and branched to the ground.

ARTFULLY NATURALISTIC

Gardens

"Remember that the most beautiful things in the world are
the most useless: peacocks and lilies, for instance."

JOHN RUSKIN

The garden designers widely credited with pioneering and promoting naturalistic planting styles are William Robinson and Gertrude Jekyll. These two influential figures created one of the most loved—and enduring—planting styles, which emerged in conjunction with the Arts and Crafts movement. More than almost any others who have practiced garden design, they have influenced the way gardens are seen and made to this day. In spite of the tendency of design trends to shift and change, naturalistic, cottage-style gardening with mixed borders has remained prevalent throughout Europe and North America. The style has evolved and changed somewhat over the last hundred and twenty-five years in important ways, to be sure, yet it is still exalted as one of the triumphs of our collective aesthetic heritage. It reflects cultural ideas about the most aesthetically pleasing ways to control nature without

seeming to do so, and also developed during a time when the British Empire could fuel the human passion for collecting exotic "new" species. Like the bowerbird, we are naturally curious and seek to make beautiful structures out of what we can find around us.

THEORIES OF COMPOSITION

The original theory behind the naturalistic style of garden design is that plants from all corners of the earth can and should be brought together and used in any climate where they can physically thrive. Coupled with this is an aesthetic of informal plant compositions that reference a painterly concept of nature. Although naturalistic plantings can be applied to an entire garden, they are most usually seen as perennial or mixed borders. These have been created and interpreted the world

Hydrangea paniculata 'Tardiva' adds inviting white blooms to a lane in late summer. Loose plantings edge the rest of the drive, lending it an informal mood. Clump irises and ferns in the distance give a vertical accent to the mounding forms that dominate the bulk of this Hoerr Schaudt planting.

LEFT: *Stachys monieri* 'Hummelo,' a variety developed by Piet Oudolf and named for the town where he lives, is a dependable summer-flowering perennial. Here it is paired with *Carex pensylvanica* and *Amsonia hubrictii* by Hoerr Schaudt. The way they are interplanted gives the impression that they all sprang up spontaneously, though each is native to a different habitat.

OPPOSITE: An arching canopy of redbuds shades a seating area while also serving as an understory to larger oaks high above; they bring a more suitable and inviting scale to this space. In turn, they are underplanted with *Astilbe chinensis* var. *taquetii* 'Superba' and *Hydrangea arborescens* 'Annabelle,' which tie the area into the larger landscape as seen in the distance.

RIGHT: A rustic wall, the sculptural seedheads of *Astilbe chinensis* var. *taquetii* 'Superba,' the last blooms of *Hydrangea arborescens* 'Annabelle,' and the open branches of a spruce create a nostalgic scene that invokes a woodland's edge in late summer. Hoerr Schaudt is very effective at creating strong moods in its projects.

over, but it is often forgotten that the Georgian Revival and Edwardian styles provided their first frameworks.

William Robinson (1838–1935) was an Irish gardener, botanist, and journalist. He was famous for being grouchy and opinionated to a fault, so he eventually turned to ways of making a living besides designing gardens for clients. He published books and magazines wherein he advocated for bringing the beauty of natural habitats into the garden via informal plantings and the use of diverse collections of hardy plants. He disliked Victorian pattern gardens where nature was suppressed and plants were meticulously managed. He was a very prodigious writer. He authored the influential book *The Wild Garden,* and *The English Flower Garden*, published in 1833, is still in print today after some twenty-plus editions. He wrote from experience in his own garden at Gravetye Manor, which visitors can now experience as a four-star bed-and-breakfast.

Gertrude Jekyll (1843–1932) was a prodigious gardener, craftswoman, photographer, plant breeder, writer, and garden designer. She is most recognized for her painterly approach to colorful flower borders—she placed more emphasis on the decorative aspects of planting design than Robinson. This was perhaps a natural inclination for her, having trained in art and art theory with John Ruskin, the leading art critic of the Victorian era. Records of pilgrimages to her garden at Munstead Wood present a who's who of the greatest names in twentieth-century garden design: Beatrix Farrand, Mien Ruys, Vita Sackville-West, Graham Stuart Thomas, and countless others. Her most famous book,

Aster divaricatus and Christmas ferns spill over cleft bluestone walls along the edge of the outdoor amphitheater at the National Cathedral in Washington, D.C., by Michael Vergason. The planting creates an effective transition between the architectural space and the woodland that surrounds it.

Colour Schemes for the Flower Garden, was a recipe book and technical explanation of how to repeat her romantic and painterly style plant combinations. After the success of *Colour Schemes*, she also wrote more than twenty other books on the crafts and architecture of her beloved Surrey. Her books contain whole treatises on roses, lilies, and woodland plants. She wrote books to encourage children to garden, a catalog of the best artifacts to collect for the garden, how to arrange cut flowers, and more. She also tried her hand at photography, painting, quilting, woodworking, pottery, and other arts and crafts. Jekyll was woman of deep experience who had a true passion for the decorative arts, and she was perpetually interested in how her ideals and theories of beauty could be transferred to her love and livelihood—gardening and garden-making. She was also noted for being generous with those who took the time to come see her.

Jekyll and Robinson fostered a new set of ideas that traveled the world and appealed to both the wealthy and the poor alike. To embrace the naturalistic style of planting, all that was needed was a passion for plants and an impulse to arrange them in a pleasing way that reflected a romanticized view of nature. Many contemporary garden designers and landscape architects continue to interpret this approach today.

Two major creative infusions of ideas have evolved the original tenets of naturalistic planting: creating multiseason gardens and making them more ecologically sensitive. Jekyll thought a garden should be arranged by season, and created a collection of garden rooms made for rotating interest throughout the calendar year. Pamela Schwerdt (1931–2009) and Sibylle Kreutzberger—the female gardening couple Vita Sackville-West hired to garden for her at her beloved Sissinghurst in Kent—later changed that notion. Although these two brilliant British gardeners are not well known outside their own country, many have experienced their work at Sissinghurt, which

they continued to maintain on behalf of the National Trust from 1962 to 1991.

Visitors flocked to Sissinghurst after it became public, and Schwerdt and Kreutzberger began to slowly make its renowned garden rooms, each of which had formerly been arranged to peak during a specific season, multiseasonal in order to keep more of the garden attractive to more people more of the time. They did not want to disappoint the visitors by limiting their experience to part of the grounds or to only one garden at a given time, so they skillfully built on Sackville-West's original themed spaces by introducing flowers for every season in each subspace.

Beth Chatto (b. 1923) is a British garden designer, plantswoman, and author who is credited with introducing ecological considerations into this naturalistic style. Rather than complaining about difficult growing conditions like dry soil, sun exposure, too much shade, wet areas, stiff clay, or the dreaded English chalk, Chatto worked to find plants that would succeed in various conditions. She also started a nursery and is a prodigious writer. Like Jekyll and Robinson, she thoroughly explains her philosophical underpinnings in her texts

LEFT: Over one hundred twenty-five years after Jekyll and Robinson pioneered the cottage style, Allan Summers of Rodney Robinson Landscape Architects has designed a nostalgic garden to surround a stone outbuilding. The interplay of deciduous and evergreen shrubs; the backdrop of spruce, birch, and crab apple; and the drift of Autumn Joy sedum create a romantic mood. This is a prime example of why the cottage style is still associated with an idealized interpretation of nature.

RIGHT: The only embellishment a rustic garage needs is a white Baby Wing begonia, perfect in its simplicity against the rustic architecture of the garage.

Rodney Robinson chose to include Virginia cedars (*Juniperus virginiana*) in this garden,
an interesting move since they are rarely used in residential applications—but are a superbly
durable tree. Here they receive an underplanting of deciduous hollies and fountain grasses
in full bloom, indicating that the crisp autumn is about to turn to winter.

and then provides practical instructions on what will work, plant by plant. This represents an evolved approach to the original concept of what a naturalistic garden should be, and is suited to today's concerns with ecology and environmentalism.

CONTEMPORARY APPROACHES

Designing cottage gardens expertly takes many years, despite how wild or casual they may look to the untrained eye. Only garden designers who spend hours acutally gardening, collecting plants, and studying horticulture can learn how to grow them, anticipate what their failings and strong attributes are likely to be, and develop a practiced eye for intriguing details. It takes trial and error. Few gardens designed in the cottage style can be achieved at installation from a paper plan. Success requires a deep knowledge of plants, horticultural confidence gained from having both studied and tested plant combinations, and a design aesthetic cultivated through years of practice.

Douglas Hoerr, a designer and principal at Hoerr Schaudt Landscape Architects in Chicago, Illinois, studied with Beth Chatto. He is able to practice fluently across several planting styles, but excels at the naturalistic cottage style. Unique to his work is his ability to use many plant types in a truly integrated way; his compositions include a full ecology of trees, shrubs, perennials, grasses, and layers of bulbs. Most garden designers are most comfortable working within one group of plants, but Hoerr Schaudt gardens are multiseasonal, ecologically sensitive, and well balanced. This is exemplified in their Winnetka, Illinois, private garden. Several local stones are arranged into patterned low walls that create the framework for the garden. A wide selection of trees and larger-scaled shrubs delineate the

ABOVE: The saffron foliage of old man's beard (*Chionanthus virginicus*) and Autumn Joy sedum create a unique color combination that surrounds a bench, revealing how Allan Summers brings his training in horticulture, art, and landscape architecture together.

BELOW: Leaves from a river birch blow across a stone terrace lined with drifts of fountain grasses and *Hydrangea paniculata* 'Limelight,' and set with a pair of Adirondack chairs that beckon for visitors to soak up the low rays of autumn sunlight.

TOP TO BOTTOM: Christine Ten Eyck uses Mexican plum underplanted with Turk's cap (*Malvaviscus arboreus* var. *drummondii*) to frame a view to a deliciously secluded residence. Arching Bamboo Muhly and American beauty-berry frame a contemporary water feature. Plants with loose habits spill out over an expanse of gravel to give this garden a casual and naturalistic feel.

divisions between different programmatic areas of the garden, and a rich under-planting of deciduous and evergreen shrubs used in conjunction with perennials creates a tapestry of vegetation that feels of an appropriate scale and character for domestic comfort. Hoerr uses both rare and common plants to great effect, with an emphasis on form and texture. He is neither a plant snob nor a collector, rather he is a strong designer with a deep knowledge of plants and adept at adapting them to different uses.

Designer Michael Vergason is a minimalist at heart; his projects are strong and clean, and all feature an original structure. His work is extraordinarily subtle although he mainly uses native plants in what at first appear to be straight-forward combinations. His fern-and-aster planting along the top of the outdoor amphithe-ater at the National Cathedral in Washington, D.C., is one of the more complex he has executed. It suits the setting well—a sloped site in a wooded area that features bluestone risers, turf seats, and converging semicircular forms that meet and overlap with slight asymmetry at the central stairs. The white asters and ferns are a simple but attractive combination that contrast nicely with the stonework and enliven the edges of a space intended for heavy pedestrian use.

Rodney Robinson and Allan Summers of Rodney Robinson Landscape Architects in Wilmington, Delaware, have designed many public and private gardens, includ-ing many estates. Robinson studied agriculture, plant science, and horticulture as well as landscape architecture. Summers studied art and was trained as a gardener

RIGHT: Ten Eyck gardens are often framed by crisp, modern architecture; to counter it she often uses plants with a soft form, sparingly. This garden room consequently feels embraced by plants but not overwhelmed by them.

LEFT: A contemporary water feature framed by switch grass, four-nerve daisies, and Mexican buckeye. The mixed planting encloses the lawn, giving the space a natural-feeling border.

Viburnum x *carlcephalum* repeated as a motif in a mixed planting by Keith LeBlanc gives structure and scale to a garden on Cape Cod. The white, globe-shaped flowers are a strong element that visually separates the garden from the surrounding landscape of deciduous trees in the distance.

at Longwood. At the Walker Residence, featured here, both of those backgrounds influence the final garden. Summers used grasses and large groups of sedums and other perennials to create a landscape that is naturalistic but also boldly composed. An extensive use of grasses is often associated with German garden design, but Americans have embraced them as well. Grasses reveal their kinetic potential in even the slightest wind and catch light with their fine texture. They are useful in combination with plants of more rounded and static forms to add panache or, more specifically, vertical accents. A skilled designer must also have the discipline to use plants in combinations that serve nearby built forms in a manner that maintains interest in all seasons. Plants, like all other elements of design, carry certain connotations—the use of hollies, lilacs, crabapples, sugar maples, and other plants that "feel" old-fashioned are appropriate for a landscape that surrounds a historic stone farmhouse and stone landscape features. Most of the woody plants are deciduous, and therefore contribute to a sense of age as they progress through the seasons. Too often, landscapes are evergreen-heavy. Simply put, the changing seasons should be celebrated.

Like many practitioners, Keith LeBlanc combines old and new ideas; his style could perhaps best be described as "transitional," which is very much in vogue right now in architecture and interior design. Keith has provided a strong, crisp frame for his Pamet Valley garden in Massachusetts. The hardscape elements include an almost minimalist, contemporary use of traditional materials, open rectilinear fences, and decking in combination with bluestone terraces. His plantings, however, rely on hedges and a loose infill of flowering plants to contrast with that strict framework and to soften the experience of the overall garden spaces, a technique derived directly from Edwardian borders.

Though the naturalistic style was developed in the temperate climates of England and is most often interpreted in America's Mid-Atlantic and northern states, its precepts adapt equally well to tropical, subtropical, and even arid climates. Current practitioners including Christine

New Dawn roses spill unchecked over the garden wall, softening the architectural element. Walker's Low catmint, which fronts it, is a mainstay for summer flowers and animates the area with the buzz of bees; it is often trimmed back hard after flowering to encourage a second, late-summer bloom. Bamboo grass is allowed to spill onto the pool deck to give a wild feel to the garden.

Snow can bring unique quietude to a garden; experiencing it can be powerful, so gardens in climates where show is inevitable are best designed with wintertime visits in mind. When lined with snow, the branches of deciduous trees and shrubs add mesmerizing dimension and an appreciation for the seasons that a garden dominated by evergreens cannot provide.

ABOVE: Los Angeles's mild climate allows temperate, tropical, and desert plants to grow together in one garden, and Elysian Landscapes emphasizes the lush possibilities beguilingly in this courtyard next to an Isabel Marant store. The trees are Chinese elm and olive—species from opposite sides of the world. *Agave attenuata* and *Monstera deliciosa*, a houseplant in most other parts of the country, give an exotic character to the garden. A wall clad in Algerian ivy at once greens and accentuates the architecture, and *Liriope gigantea* borders the entry path.

OPPOSITE: Bold rosettes of *Agave attenuata*, along with the other, smaller agaves, ground this planting scheme. The fuzzy-leaved *Kalanchoe beharensis* and the vertical cactus *Lemaireocereus marginatus* provide further structure, which is knitted together with senecio and *Dianella caerulea* Cassa Blue.

Ten Eyck, who practices in the South and desert Southwest, and Judy Kameon of Elysian Landscapes, based in California, have effectively adapted the cottage style to their respective zones. Ten Eyck brings a subtlety to the style that is comfortable, easy, and makes her gardens sit well in the region. Namely, she uses native plants extensively, but mixes them with exotics to achieve a selection of softly textured and billowing forms. Ten Eyck, like LeBlanc, tends to design a crisp, architectural framework for a garden and to then create a counterpoint to that with "soft" plants. Kameon has a flare for the dramatic and a deep sense of romanticism which, perhaps ironically, she expresses perfectly well with prickly succulents. The dimension other designers achieve with casual massings and loose tufts of perennials she matches with the bold forms of a variety of desert species.

On the opposite coast, Raymond Jungles practices primarily with the native species of Florida as his palette. He first became known for a bold and graphic planting style inspired by his long friendship with Roberto Burle Marx, but his deep knowledge

ABOVE: In L.A., flowering aloes are the harbingers of winter. Their blooms are typically orange or red, like this Aloe 'Cynthia Giddy,' and they often attract humming-birds to a garden.

RIGHT: Aloe, artemisia, *Salvia* 'Mystic Spires Blue,' agave, and more are all combined here in a subtropical take on Gertrude Jekyll's theory of combining plants native to different lands in artistic ways.

and obvious love of plants have given him the confidence to move in a more natu-ralistic—indeed wild—direction when his projects call for it. He will often mix the two styles, however, inferring nature's hand by massing native plants in dense concentra-tions and then juxtaposing them with a strong architectural or hardscape element. He has the advantage of having large-leaved tropical plants and palms at his disposal, and uses them to create lush, all-encompassing, and exuberant spaces.

ENDURING APPEAL

The romantic and naturalistic use of plants first adopted in England by Gertrude Jekyll and William Robinson has served as an extraordinary point of departure for later related styles. Their approach has been both followed slavishly and reacted against over the last one hundred twenty-five years—notably by modernists, who thought of it as "classist" due to the skill and funding needed to maintain the large country house

ABOVE: Tropical plants embrace the entry to a home with a complex array of foliage. Raymond Jungles builds the planting scheme in layers, from the low fireworks of bromeliads *Neoregelia* 'McWilliamsii,' which first greet visitors, to an eye-height palm and the dramatic dark leaves of *Leea coccinea* 'Rubra.' A heart-shaped philodendron 'McDowell' provides an accent.

OPPOSITE: Nature's variety is on full display in a courtyard at the same home. Under the shade of a gumbo limbo tree, a philodendron 'McDowell', the fan palm *Corypha utan*, and the cycad *Ceratozamia mexicana* provide structure and eye-height interest while meandering drifts of various *Neoregelia* species border a unique path of rectangular pavers.

gardens that provided the best-known examples of the style. Elaborate plantings were eventually also viewed as wasteful by the middle and lower classes, and were seen as encumbering to those of the upper classes who wished to embrace a life focused on leisure and recreational pursuits. In spite of all this, amateur and professional gardeners across the country today still aspire to create naturalistic gardens and bountiful borders, despite the gargantuan commitment of time required to learn enough about plants to design them convincingly.

To master this style, a designer or amateur gardener must embrace the physical act of gardening as much as the study of plants and the theories behind naturalistic design. Many of the best designers working in this

Pavers of travertine floating in gravel suggest intimate, enveloped spaces for seating arrangements amid layered plantings. The burbling of the adjacent fountain and pool reach these areas as well.

medium have ended up at public gardens or on private estates, where they generally have access to financial support and long timelines for implementing ideas. The style is as much about process as product, so it attracts plantsmen and women who are addicted to endless trial and error or, more precisely, to constant refinement. It takes great skill to maintain cottage-style gardens, and gardening this way is a never-ending journey—but one that yields countless joys in many small successes along the way.

The silver foliage of a *Conocarpus erectus* laps over an architectural fountain in a garden by Raymond Jungles. It is underplanted with the philodendron 'McDowell,' a strong counterpoint to the other rectilinear features present. Tropical water lilies bring the garden forward, across the water and around the stepping-stones, giving dimension to the landscape.

3

Graphic ||||||||||

PLANTING DESIGN

"Gardening is not nature—

it is a cultural bias imposed on nature."

ANONYMOUS

T he definition of the graphic planting style is somewhat straightforward: the use of plants in large blocks and, for the most part, in monocultural massings to create a graphic effect on the landscape. This style can create dynamic tensions in the garden by using plants in a way that has more to do with art, perhaps, than with the familiar naturalistic style that is traditional. Cubism and surrealism had a strong influence on the development of this style and served as the inspiration for using plants themselves as an expressive material, like paint, to create large swaths of color and texture. Block planting as a technique is immensely useful for creating "modern" gardens where plants appear in either sweeping curves or clearly defined shapes.

Graphic or "block style" planting can also be dramatic when plants are arranged in a patterned way. The dynamics of this style can be amplified by creating strong contrasts between individual

LEFT: Society garlic is a nearly forgotten edible herb with lavender flowers; once the foliage is bruised, it gives off a strong garlic odor. It is combined here by Roche+Roche with plants organized into distinct groupings of Pheasant's-tail grass, mounded lavender, and *Ceanothus* 'Joan Mirov.' The range of foliage makes the entrance to this home memorable and inviting.

ABOVE: Light that catches *Libertia* leaves magnifies their tawny pigments, which also appear in stone walls that tie the garden's framework to the plants.

PREVIOUS PAGES: Roche+Roche chose colors for this garden in Napa that would hold up well to the strong light. Copper-toned foliage on *Libertia peregrinans* flows under an olive tree, blue-green coast rosemary provides a distinctive and contrasting foreground, and the seed heads of *Miscanthus transmorrisonensis* create a high and fluid edge in the background.

Large sweeps of slender veldt grass (*Pennisetum spathiolatum*) studded with olive trees create an intriguing edge for a vineyard that gradually cedes to a nut-tree orchard. Roche+Roche tie together agriculture and designed landscape at this winery in Oakville, California, to create an experience that celebrates the Napa Valley.

blocks of plants in terms of both color and form, or introduced in a subtler way by planting species that share certain characteristics. Some of the earliest graphic gardens were created in South America with tropical plants; when the graphic movement caught on in America and was embraced in our temperate climates, perennials and grasses were used to achieve a similar effect, notably by Wolfgang Oehme and James van Sweden. They coined the name the "New American Garden" to describe the style. The earliest landscape designers to employ block planting were also looking to design gardens that would complement modernist houses built by architects such as Eero Saarinen and Oscar Niemeyer.

Brazilian landscape architect, artist, ecologist, and musician Roberto Burle Marx (1909–1994) is perhaps the man most famous for experimenting with the graphic planting style. His bold, curvilinear, graphic forms are still instantly recognizable today. Burle Marx's influence on designers and garden-makers in the second half of the twentieth century was profound. His projects clearly express his love of plants, joyful use of color, and affinity for strong form. He was an avid plant researcher and collected many species, particularly from his native lands, and he was an early proponent of conservation, including advocacy for preservation of the rain forests. Burle Marx was also notoriously disciplined about his plant selections; their apparent simplicity, stemming from a seemingly minimalist color palette and simple forms, do not mean that his designs are not sophisticated. Burle Marx's knowledge of plants was expansive and diverse, and he used plants like the colors of paint on a canvas. His simpler designs often included fifty different kinds of plants—larger projects contained in excess of a hundred varieties. His encyclopedic knowledge of plants helped him achieve precise effects in terms of color, texture, and form. He embraced diversity, but tempered it with a strong sense of composition and design intent. The fusion between

ABOVE: Light and shade play across slender veldt grass to create a simple but intriguing entry sequence to the tasting rooms at a California winery.

RIGHT: Mediterranean rosemary is well-adapted to Northern California. Here, Roche+Roche edge an expanse of it with a grass that features contrasting textures, creating a strong pattern in the landscape that also draws the eye to the distant horizon.

Russian sage is a dependable plant in all climates but the Deep South; here Roche+Roche use it as a foil to the gray-green foliage of rosemary. The finely cut leaves of both plants complement the intricately textured stone facade of this home near Yountville, California.

LEFT: A carpet of *Artemisia* 'Powis Castle'—a drought-tolerant and dependable ground cover—is used here with *Miscanthus* and *Calamagrostis*. The pale, subtle colors in the landscape merge with the group of white umbrellas to create a setting that is readable and modern.

RIGHT: *Calamagrostis* x *acutiflora* 'Karl Foerster' is a popular grass due to its straw-colored seed heads and board-straight vertical growth habit, which give it immediate presence in any landscape. Here it creates a striking pairing with a weeping willow waiting to shield a lucky siesta-taker from the California sun. Mounding blue grama grass (*Bouteloua gracilis* 'Blonde Ambition') showing its late-summer seed heads and a winding gravel path add softness and curve to the composition.

One of the first major commissions Oehme, van Sweden received was for the Federal Reserve in Washington, D.C., some twenty years ago; they were recently invited to update it. This landscape introduced a new style of planting—the graphic style—to American landscape architects. In this section of the garden, Knock Out roses add color and structure to grasses and herbaceous plantings and lead the eye to a fountain.

Context is key for establishing appropriate plant use. Neatly pruned shrubs line the area immediately adjacent to the 1974 concrete facade of the William McChesney Martin, Jr. Building; the restrained characters work well together here, but as the garden recedes into the landscape beyond, it grows gradually more free-form.

art and landscape is inseparable in his work. His landscapes clearly celebrate life and capture and embrace modern design in a buoyant way.

In North America, early modernists who embraced the graphic planting style included Thomas Church (1902–1978), whose early work included El Novillero, a famous garden in Sonoma with an iconic curvilinear swimming pool. His interest in modernism was passed to Robert Royston (1918–2008), Garrett Eckbo (1910–2000), Dan Kiley (1912–2004), and James Rose (1913–1991), who all embraced modern landscape

Switch grass, Russian sage, and Knock Out roses in strongly defined masses read well from a distance and are durable for a heavily trafficked urban setting. The partners at Oehme, van Sweden continue to embrace the style of their founders, but also adapt their plant choices with the times as new and dependable plants are introduced.

Large and dome-shaped viburnums add a clean, bold structure to looser
plantings in front of the Marriner S. Eccles Federal Reserve Board Building;
they also add a formality and height that complement both the stately
architecture and the impressive nearby fountain.

On a sunny day, the essential oils in the foliage of *Pycnanthemum* perfume the air with a crisp, minty fragrance, providing urban inhabitants with a welcome reminder of nature. The mass plantings provide bands of color and texture that suit the monumental scale of the government offices adjacent.

This garden by Oehme, van Sweden feels timeless and familiar now, although when it was installed it created and established a new style in America. Liriope, switch grass, roses, and low-growing yews planted in a graphic way reflect the solidity of the nearby architecture while also softening it at ground level

design and employed a graphic planting style, although often with very simple plant compositions. All were contemporaries and in communication with one another; they developed a new aesthetic based on low maintenance needs, a modern design vocabulary, and they believed that well-designed public projects could truly make life better for the middle class that emerged after World War II. Embracing the modernist design mantra "form follows function," plants in modernist landscapes were most often selected for spatial delineation, scale, or environmental modifications such as sun protection and visual appeal.

EVOLUTION OF THE STYLE

The graphic style of planting has become exceedingly popular, although it has evolved and now encompasses various interpretations. This style offers several advantages: it creates a strong aesthetic that is bold, free-form, and highly emotive; masses of plants are easier to maintain than other more traditional arrangements for gardens because without the complexity of a highly patterned arrangement of plants, less-skilled labor can

ABOVE: Raymond Jungles builds up layers of tropical plants in sweeping masses along an entry drive to a residence in South Florida. The pothos, most familiar as a houseplant, features beguiling asymmetrical cream stripes that sparkle in the sunlight, adding variety to the myriad of greens.

RIGHT: Raymond Jungles is renowned for his extensive use of bromeliads; here abundant masses of low *Neoregelia* 'Jill' border a path that leads to an arbor and a garden room beyond. Tall stalks of *Bambusa chungii* shade the gateway, while the waving leaves of cycad *Ceratozamia mexicana* beckon from the side.

Loquats and stately palms relate well to the scale of a two-story house. The
sweep of crimson daylilies adds a welcoming splash of color to the entry.

For the Brazilian Garden at the Naples Botanical
Garden, Raymond Jungles floated the captivating
water lilies *Victoria* x 'Longwood Hybrid' over a
beguiling black pool. Silver *Vriesea* along the edge
of the pond matches the scale of the water lilies'
4-to-8-foot round leaves, while lower-growing red-
leaved bromeliads relate back to the lilies' edges.

Hoerr Schaudt planted sedum and prairie dropseed in Mondrian-esque configurations for this roof garden in Chicago, making it a treat for all those in adjacent buildings to gaze upon.

LEFT: *Calamagrostis* is remarkably hardy—it performs equally well in zone 8 or zone 5. Here it serves as one of the more vertical elements among the plants chosen for a green roof.

BELOW: Sedums in gray, pink, coral, red, and purple, along with *Allium schoenoprasum* 'Forescate'—a perennial as opposed to a bulbous variety—and feather reed-grass *Calamagrostis* x *acutiflora* 'Karl Foerster' create a cubic pattern that is compelling to look down on from higher in the building.

be taught to manage individual species; plants in drifts or masses are easily understood by the viewer; and, finally, graphic planting is a perfect counterpoint to the bold form of modern and contemporary architecture.

Piet Oudolf, a contemporary Dutch garden designer best known for his work on the High Line in New York and at the Lurie Garden at Millennium Park in Chicago, used yew sculpted into wave forms as a terminus and focal point in his personal garden, Hummelo, near Arnhem in the Netherlands. This was an exciting use of a large block of plants to create movement simultaneously and in three dimensions. By thinking of hedges in this way, the opportunities for design are only limited by our imagination.

Wirtz International, a Belgian landscape design firm run by Jacques Wirtz and his two sons, Martin and Peter, has a different vocabulary but works to create equally striking effects. They are renowned for their use of clipped hornbeams, beech trees, yews, boxwood, and other plants in a similarly graphic manner to create a dizzying array of different shapes and forms. They have led a movement to reembrace clipped forms in the modern garden.

The firm Oehme, van Sweden, located in Washington D.C., was founded by James van Sweden (1935–2013), and Wolfgang Oehme (1930–2011), in 1977. Together they popularized New American Garden landscape design, a style that eschews manicured lawns and foundation plantings but promotes naturalistic landscapes planted in a graphic style; these often explode exuberantly with grasses and wildflowers. For example, most of a garden might be planted in a graphic style, but near intensively used areas more complex or naturalistic sections might be planted, which promotes closer inspection on the part of the viewer. Large masses of plants also simplify maintenance; inserting beds with more intricate planting schemes into a garden that is predominantly composed of larger groups of plants adds depth and dimension but manages the expense of care. Oehme, van Sweden is adept with all types of plants, and mixes them in effective and thoughtful ways. Their style changes and morphs to fit each project and site as well. The graphic planting style for the Federal Reserve in Washington, D.C. and the meadows of the New York Botanical Garden's new Native Plant Garden respond uniquely to each site's intended use. The firm's current partners have maintained this style even as they embrace—and create—new trends.

CONTEMPORARY PRACTITIONERS

Raymond Jungles is a landscape architect based in Miami. His early influences include Roberto Burle Marx and Mexican architect Luis Barragán (1902–1988), who was known for injecting strong, sculptural planes of color into the landscape. The high-contrast, ebullient signature style employed by Burle Marx is difficult to achieve in most temperate regions of the country, but works well in subtropical and tropical climates. Jungles has interpreted and expanded on his work, and has become known for using a range of plants with bold colors and sculptural forms such as all types of palms, bromeliads, tropical figs, philodendrons, various vines, and coleus—a perennial in a tropical climate. He often creates nuanced schemes based primarily on tones of green, for example, rather than saturated, colored foliage. He relies on contrasting textures and forms to add interest. The effect is distinctive; his compositions create a feeling of being enveloped by a landscape slightly denser and more varied than what Mother Nature herself might have created.

The Chicago Parks District adopted block planting for spaces along Michigan Avenue, just east of the Chicago Art Institute. Here Korean feather-reed grass (*Calamagrostis brachytricha*) and little bluestem (*Schizachryium scoparium*) are faced with a sedge to create a modern prairie in the heart of the city.

Hoerr Schaudt, based in Chicago, has become known for its inventive use of plants. Their projects often include diverse selections of durable varieties, and they are confident designers with the ability to work across several styles. Their roof gardens use a necessarily limited selection of plants but still achieve strikingly graphic results. The design featured here is based on rectilinear compositions, which read well from the higher floors of adjacent buildings, complement the surrounding architecture, and are easy to maintain. This last point is critical, considering the scale of the project and the effort it takes to manage. Principal Douglas Hoerr has a deep knowledge of plants that he uses to achieve unexpected combinations, such as perennial onions in combination with grasses. By limiting the form of the plants to grasslike species, the overall composition remains crisp and subtle.

Another application of the graphic style in Hoerr Schaudt's work is along Michigan Avenue, just west of the Art Institute of Chicago, in a series of beds along the street maintained by the Chicago Parks District. North American native plants are combined with Asian grasses in a powerful, bold, and colorful way. The plantings vary in height from eighteen inches to five feet, with a color palette from variegated yellow to blue, rust, and all shades of green. These beds use a narrowly defined texture in a rich and impactful way. The taller selections align well with such a large-scaled space, but the stylized prairie plantings reference the region and make the public space along the sidewalk more human-scaled. The soft, kinetic grasses are an amazing contrast to the hard urban setting. Simply put, they are daring and refreshing, and all passersby can recognize them as such.

A project Land Morphology has been privileged to work on is Silas Mountsier's garden in Nutley, New Jersey. He is a collector of garden objects and sculptures, and

Deschampsia and switch grass are added to the mix to create a pattern of amber waves that give eye-height movement noticeable from the sidewalk—or from the car.

the garden is planted in an artistic, graphic style that features a broad range of plants including trees, shrubs, herbaceous perennials, and grasses. The strength and simplicity of the design include enough diversity for interest but, most important, create a pleasant backdrop for the garden objects. The garden art is sometimes striking and deserving of a focal point: a bronze cow, for example, is placed "grazing" on the lawn against a backdrop of like hornbeams and bamboo grass whimsically shaped to evoke hay bales. Other pieces are surrounded with plantings that support them but do not necessarily make them stand out. Though the main color palette of the foliage used throughout the estate is medium to dark green, a number of blue and yellow foliage plants are introduced for impact; the entire garden is a celebration of dramatic contrasts.

The overall garden is calm and intellectually stimulating, a result that stems from a twenty-year dedication to its construction between the designer, Silas, and his partner, Graeme Hardie. It is a highly personal place that friends, family, and visitors respond to in emotional ways.

Nelson Byrd Woltz's design for the Citygarden in St. Louis maximizes the full range of plants that will grow well in that climate. Most of the perennials used in the project

LEFT: In the Mountsier garden in Nutley, New Jersey, Land Morphology planted 10,000 plugs of bamboo grass in four swaths of color along a rolling berm and punctuated it with square pillars of clipped hornbeam. When the wind blows, the lighthearted effect is of looking at a giant caterpillar.

RIGHT: White Bourbon roses add a highlight between concrete walls that pierce the berm of grasses, drawing the eye to a sight line from the guesthouse into the heart of the garden.

Carex morrowii 'Ice Ballet,' with its white variegated leaves, gives the impression of sunlight even in shady areas. The simple border of it along the path creates a strong plane that complements the narrow-growing copper beeches. This little-used, spring flowering, woodland plant from China (*Disporum flavum*) related to Solomon's seal is worth searching out—it is durable and unique.

RIGHT: The weeping branches and distinct leaves of Hearts of Gold redbud are underplanted with All Gold bamboo grass; both catch the wind to create delicate movement.

BELOW: A long massing of *Carex morrowii* 'Ice Ballet' leads up the path between hornbeams into the garden beyond while Dainty the bronze cow watches over all. The simple plantings allow the sculpture to take center stage. The horizontal shrub to the upper right of her head masks a small platform that comes as a surprise and allows a visitor to see many of the garden rooms on the property at once.

Solar Cascade goldenrod is one of the
very best varieties on the market. Here
in St. Louis's Citygarden, Nelson Byrd
Woltz used it to add late-summer
interest behind a popular interactive
water feature.

are in fact selections of various prairie plants. Though the planting motif is distinctly modern, the reference to the character of native plants is apparent. The design uses big blocks of flowering perennials to visually excite and, as described previously, the block or graphic planting has the benefit of being an easier style to maintain. The park is a fantastic intersection of art, strong built forms, interactive features, and a masterful use of plants to make a compelling landscape that the residents of St. Louis have embraced and use fully. It is exciting to see beautifully detailed structures like the water feature, which references the Mississippi River, and sculptures by Tom Otterness, Tony Smith, and others, energized and integrated with the exquisite use of plants—the living part of the gardens—to attract diverse visitors.

Gustafson Guthrie Nichol (GGN), is an award-winning firm headquartered in Seattle. Their landscape for the Bill and Melinda Gates Foundation represents an evolution of the graphic style of planting. The landscape is conceived in blocks but, rather than designating a single species for each area, the designers have introduced two or more

ABOVE: Nelson Byrd Woltz has melded the surrounding prairie with the historic fabric of St. Louis in Citygarden. This interactive art park is planted in a bold block style, which is low maintenance and holds interest in every season. *Rudbeckia subtomentosa* 'Henry Eilers' along with a gold-variegated rush, capture the warm light of late September and provide a setting for the sculpture *Big Suit* by Erwin Wurm.

LEFT: The delicacy of Black-eyed Susans is enhanced by a limestone wall; their blooms soften the approach to a monumental sculpture by Mark di Suvero.

Pinocchio celebrates the fact that he is now a boy in a large planting of Henry Eilers Black-eyed Susans. The cheerful yellow flowers emphasize the emotion projected by Jim Dine's sculpture.

Nelson Byrd Woltz underplanted a ceiling of shadblow with Lenten roses. The dappled shade and low greenery make an appealing place for a quick lunch during the workweek. *Calamintha*, which blooms for months, finishes the sunnier end of the space and draws the eye to a sculpture by Jack Youngerman.

OPPOSITE: Wedge-shaped blocks of grasses and sedges in the courtyard at the Bill & Melinda Gates Foundation in Seattle give the building's plaza a sense of expansiveness. Gustafson Guthrie Nichol combined native shrubs *Rosa nutkana* and *Mahonia aquifolium* with grasses *Molinia caerulea* and *Miscanthus sinensis* 'Purpurascens' and the rush *Juncus effusus*.

RIGHT: Rushes break up the water's surface and provide a modern-looking foreground that complements the architecture by NBBJ.

BELOW: *Camassia*, a Pacific Northwest native, is planted in a large mass to add color and dimension to the Bill & Melinda Gates Foundation campus.

different plant species in each block. It is immediately understood that the planting design is meant to be graphic and architectural in nature, but the mixing of plants versus planting a monoculture in a given area softens the effect, adds diversity, and increases seasonal interest. The aquatic planting in the water feature—which also doubles as a filtration pond for the water captured on site as building and plaza runoff—is designed simply, with a large block of native reeds that function as a strong design element in the very urban courtyard between the buildings.

Roche+Roche are a husband-and-wife team; his strength is structure, she works up the detailed designs. Plantings that are adapted to the Northern California climate and a heavy use of grasses characterize their work. Attention to slight variations in foliage color and texture make their designs, which emphasize simplicity, effective.

Andrea Cochran, another designer based in the San Francisco area, always starts with strong and innovative landforms. Her use of construction materials and a restrained palette of plants reinforce the built elements, then flesh out the overall structure. She uses plants to support her constructed topography, choosing them carefully to impart a sense of movement to the dynamic geometries she develops.

Andrea Cochran paired blocks of Japanese maples with a Cor-Ten steel planter/bench; the color combination is striking in fall. As the trees mature, they will continue to fill the space and have an even stronger presence in this plaza that surrounds the Energy Biosciences Building at the University of California, Berkeley.

LEFT: Landscape design must partner with time; these coastal redwoods will eventually reach the roof of the building to make a vertical block of greenery against the its rhythmic facade, and the Japanese maples will fit snugly just under the windows. Their colors already enhance the built form.

BELOW: A line of aloes in a low planter creates a strong horizontal line. The repetition makes the space calm and anchored. As more of them come into flower, the effect against the glass wall will be captivating.

Her work's strength and her edgy aesthetics that adapt well to today's tastes make it distinctive.

Jeffrey Carbo's work is strongly architectural, making it a natural pairing for projects featuring contemporary architecture with strong lines. He is based in Louisiana and shows a bias toward native plants, although he does not characterize himself as a purist. Often bold and geometric lines carry from a site's architecture out into his planting concepts, enhancing both at once. Various designers prefer groups of plants over others—Carbo uses the whole range of plants in his projects and knits his landscapes together in rational but lush ways.

LEFT: Softly tufted expanses of a mix of emerald grasses (*Koeleria macrantha*, *Deschampsia elongata*, and *Festuca rubra*) contrast with perforated, weathered, Cor-Ten steel retaining walls designed by Andrea Cochran that mediate an 11-foot change in grade between the adjacent sidewalk and the entrance to the building.

OPPOSITE: Alternating bands of steel and plants line a zigzagging, ADA-compliant pathway to the building, creating a compelling design that provides plenty of color even in early fall. The trees at the rear are Japanese maples and 'Regent' scholar's trees.

Seed heads of *Allium albopilosum* are just as striking in midsummer as they are in spring, when they are flowering. Layers of fountain grass, Mexican sage, and hyssop make the Elliott Park Campus in Seattle eye-catching from the street.

Pennisetum forms a ground for masses of saturated colors offered by perennials and annuals in summer. Waves of tulips and other bulbs are interplanted among the herbaceous plants for colorful waves in the spring.

A STYLE FOR TOMORROW

The graphic planting style is dramatic and simple, and it immediately expresses a clarity of vision. It stands for masterful site plans, strong design skills, and a deep appreciation for plants all wrapped up together to make places that people are drawn to for their beauty, refreshing outlook on garden design, and attention to interactive details. This style is evolving to include the use of green and built vertical forms and visual and circulation axes that establish strong spatial frameworks. Within these, perennials and grasses can be introduced in overall composition as "blocks" of plants, which can be established as monocultures or as matrices. These can at once reinforce the framework and contrast with built forms.

Graphic planting lends itself well to constant experimentation and change, which is key to bringing innovative ideas to the forefront. The best-designed places are those that express strong and studied techniques, and with its focus on more sustainable landscapes, ecology, and high-performance landscapes, it is likely that the graphic style may evolve to include matrices of diverse plants arranged in graphic patterns, with built and architectural features forming frames. Within these frames, designers can introduce more plant diversity and augment ecological function. Increasingly, landscape designers are eschewing architectural elements to define space and reintroducing clipped hedges, green walls, trellises laden with plants, and bosques of columnar or shaped trees. Urban spaces are becoming softer yet more sophisticated and designed for diverse users and functions while at the same time adding more consideration of temporal and ecological nuances.

Contemporary landscape architects working in this style are also using more complex palettes as their understanding of ecology grows and the benefits of diversity, habitat connectivity, conservation, and systems thinking are embraced. It is now considered desirable to create very clean, architectural spaces filled with a diverse palette of plants. High-performance landscapes are in vogue because they can respond to many programmatic desires: water retention/cleansing, pollination, habitat creation, carbon sequestration, urban agriculture, preservation of unique and/or historical species, educational imperatives, and climate change adaptation. Designers are exploring how to integrate all these performance objectives, and often returning with stunning compositions and modern landscapes that contribute to the making of exquisite places.

Various marshmallows and duckweed surround floating paths at the Shangri La Botanical Gardens in Orange, Texas. Jeffrey Carbo uses stripes of pickerel-weed to give a visual strength to the edge of the water feature. A steel-sided runner of clear, moving water is a clever detail that adds dynamism.

The triangular canopies of bald cypresses are given a strong counterpoint by upright blocks of Louisiana iris at the St. Landry Parish Visitor Information Center in Opelousas, Louisiana. The Jeffrey Carbo design draws attention to the orthogonal arrangements of the walks and a water element.

Gulf Coast muhly grass and meadow grasses create a strong sight line to the building's
entry and catch the glow from modern path lights even at dusk. The bald cypresses
used in groupings will eventually mask the roof but frame the glass curtain wall, establishing a strong interplay between landscape and architecture.

4

MEADOW

Gardens

"The living beauty of nature cannot be copied:

it can only be expressed."

PIET MONDRIAN

Recent interest in interpreting ecology artfully has led to the use of native plants in contemporary landscapes, particularly in ways that emulate to some degree how they appear in the wild. This began with Ian McHarg (1920–2001), who transmitted his ideas through teaching and extensive writing, and who has influenced the last two generations of design professionals. Phlox, black-eyed Susans, monarda, baptisia, and coneflowers are all now treated like prairie plants that have gone to finishing school—meadows are in vogue. Wild, casual plantings that often include little bluestem and switch grass also form a good aesthetic counterpoint to modern architecture because they add visual interest but not fussy adornment. Planting native landscapes—formerly a specialized skill—is growing into a more widespread craft. Meadows were usually only to be found in botanical gardens, parks, and large open-space restorations a few years ago, now they're often introduced into urban and residential projects.

A sculptural sphere receives a frame of grasses in the John Greenlee garden at CornerStone in Sonoma. Though the individual grasses have an informal, loose habit, they form a definite composition when massed into meadows. The low-growing *Festuca rubra* and the taller *Muhlenbergia lindheimeri* both draw the eye to the horizon in different ways, thereby including the borrowed landscape in the space.

Prairies and meadows are both deceptively complex ecosystems. The terms are used interchangeably in most landscape planning and the types of plants found in each natural community are substantially similar, but scale is the biggest differentiator—prairies are large and expansive and often cover many square miles while meadows are simply smaller. Each also encompasses a range of native ecological types: wet and dry meadows, meadows at varying elevations, those that grow on soils with pH extremes, and so on. This volume does not cover ecological restoration of native ecosystems, which are typically implemented on a large scale and use only locally available ecotypes of plants from the region or project site. Restoring native ecologies takes planning and often is a multiyear commitment. Ideally seeds are collected from adjacent or nearby ecosystems and propagated. This type of project is usually the domain of biologists or restoration ecologists, rather than landscape design professionals. Landscape design firms that specialize in landscape restoration, however, do exist.

The earliest "constructed" meadows were created by indigenous peoples who burned off forestland to create and maintain hunting grounds. Although meadow plantings are an environmentally sustainable form of garden, the perception that meadows are much less maintenance than conventional gardens is far from the truth. Artificially created meadows can be a rich and inspirational expression of both grasses and perennials—or forbs, as they are known in a native prairie system. Meadows are lower maintenance once established, but in most designed applications they count as a manmade ecotype.

PRACTICAL CONSIDERATIONS

Creating meadows with diverse species takes five to ten years. First, a matrix of primary species must be established; secondary species are added over time. Warm-season grasses and associated forbs are easiest to establish. They predominate in areas where summer rainfall of twenty inches or more can sustain growth even in the heat. These plants establish rapidly and crowd out invasive or undesirable species quickly.

Rudbeckia fulgida var. *deamii* is larger in all parts than 'Goldsturm' but more resistant to disease and more drought resistant. Land Morphology planted 3,000 plugs to create a monocultural meadow around the water feature in a Nutley, New Jersey, garden.

This meadow, planted with 150,000 plugs, is based on three plants: switch grass, turkeyfoot grass, and 'Fireworks' goldenrod. Monarda, baptisia, and Carolina peas are peppered throughout for spring and early summer flower. The meadow's crescendo, however, is in September when the 80,000 goldenrods are flowering. Land Morphology laid out the plants in waves to create a painterly effect of grasses and perennials.

Rehbraun switch grass, the main grass used in this meadow, is seen here in September; its pink-brown flowers create billowy masses that spill fluidly over the top of a retaining wall.

A stone outbuilding, a remnant of the original DuPont homestead, lies at the rear of an 80-acre meadow at Longwood Gardens. The scale of this undertaking to re-create what an Eastern seaboard meadow would have looked like before settlers is impressive; in autumn, the subtle coloring of the various native grasses is truly mesmerizing.

Seed heads of native grasses in autumn prove that not all beauty comes from showy blooms. The branches of a sugar maple beginning to reveal its splendid colors extend to the edge of a nearby walk, allowing visitors to immerse themselves fully in the fall surroundings.

Weeding is the most costly investment related to establishing new meadows, as they require constant attention until the native plants are established enough to outcompete the unwanted species. Drier summer climates make this process more difficult and require a longer establishment period. Cool-season grasses will predominate, though grow slowly since they go dormant in the heat of the summer as an adaptive response to climate.

Though the focus for meadows is often on the use of native plants, many designers also create meadows that include nonnative species, mixing and matching adapted plants found in meadow and prairie ecologies on other continents. For example John Greenlee, a designer based in California, uses his expertise in grass ecology to create meadows. He does not strictly interpret or practice making meadows with only North American native plants, however. He is most interested in creating beautiful places above all, and in using sustainable plants to reduce the resources required to maintain a landscape.

There are two or three main ways to install a meadow-style planting. The least expensive material cost is seeding. However, plants grown from seed take longer to establish and initially require more weeding, resulting in higher maintenance costs.

Scarlet and yellow gaillardias feature prominently in the Simpson Prairie, near Crawford, Texas, at midsummer. It is not a long-lived perennial, but seeds in great profusion to quickly colonize a landscape.

Installing plugs is more expensive, but these plants establish more rapidly so maintenance costs during establishment are proportionately less. A hybrid approach is to seed the major species and add plugs for diversity. It is critical to understand that this is a lengthy process; otherwise impatient owners will perceive the meadows as "weedy" and will be displeased with progress during the establishment phase.

It does take gardening experience and a deep knowledge of natural systems and the plants in those systems to understand how to plant in this style. One of the masters was the late gardening writer Christopher Lloyd, owner of Great Dixter in East Sussex, England. Lloyd was not stringent about the use of solely native plants. For maximum aesthetic interest, he used plants from various regions around the world that shared a similar ecology. He also established many rare and difficult species in meadows by seeding and plugging over several decades. The meadows that he created are biologically rich and can be considered the pinnacle of the form.

Meadows seeded as a design feature tend to be composed primarily of grass matrices and the more vigorous perennial species, simply because they germinate and establish quickly. A ratio of 60 percent grasses to 40 percent forbs is a good rule of thumb. The time of seeding is critical and varies by region. Germination depends on rainfall and stratification needs of the various species used. Some seeds will not germinate unless they go through a cold period, i.e., winter. Most grasses will germinate as long as there is ample water and critical temperatures. Cool-season grasses need a lower soil temperate to germinate. Lawns are typically cool-season grasses, which is why they are sown in spring and fall. Warm-season grasses need warmer soil temperatures and are typically sown in early and late summer. If a meadow is sown in late summer, however, it is important to give it time to establish so it will survive the following winter. Yarrows and coneflowers, goldenrods, milkweeds, and joe-pye weeds are easy to establish through seeding. Baptisias and most bulbous perennials are difficult to seed and therefore are often added as plugs once the primary plant community is established from seed.

It is critical to understand the ecology of the site being worked with when selecting appropriate species. Most seeded meadows fail because plant selection was not thoroughly understood and poor or no germination was achieved; if weeds invade, no

ABOVE: A prairie in the middle of New York City is an unexpected sight. Little bluestem dominates the planting on the visitor center roof at the Brooklyn Botanic Garden, designed by Weiss/Manfredi and HMWhite. The hillside opposite is planted with hophornbeams and Pennsylvania sedge. Seeing the mid-rise buildings of the surrounding city appear over the tops of waving stalks of grass makes for a memorable experience.

OPPOSITE: Rain gardens in the entry plaza to the Brooklyn Botanic Garden visitor center are planted with tupelo, Amsonia, and Shenandoah switch grass. Although their plots are diminutive, they are also planted in a loose, meadowy arrangement.

property owner will tolerate the result. Using plugs is much more expensive, but establishment is easier to control. The result is a meadow that is established more quickly, can be more diverse, and has instant impact. Soil preparation is the same—disturbance should be kept to a minimum to suppress weed seeds. Coordination with growers is required in advance so that all the species required are available at planting time. Meadows must be planned six months to a year ahead. Without planning, it is unlikely enough plants will be available. Most growers sell out quickly and each plant is on a different production schedule. With good planning, the slower-growing choices can be held and made available with the more rapid-growing crops. Warm-season plants fill in rapidly as plugs and achieve their intended effect in six to twelve months, as opposed to seeded projects, which can take two to three years. Over time, plant communities also drift and move; as a result, original plants installed as plugs will begin to self-seed. It is gratifying to watch a system become self-sustaining and take on a life of its own.

ARTFUL INTERPRETATIONS

Longwood Gardens in Delaware has opened an extraordinary meadow project encompassing 86 acres. After a road realignment, it was incorporated into the garden proper and opened to the public. For maximum impact and interest, additional forbs—perennials—were added to the extensive grasses on the site. This meadow has been in development for many years; part of the effort to integrate it with the rest of the garden focused on embedding it with plants that would flower sequentially throughout the growing season to add interest for visitors over the course of many months. New pathways, shelters, boardwalks, and unique bridges also help visitors move deep into the meadow. This, then, is not an expression of a native ecology, but an interpretation of nature that is composed to inspire. It is extraordinary to look at this great expanse and to consider the amount of dedication involved in making it a reality.

Mike Williams has been working on the Simpson Prairie near Crawford, Texas, for twenty years. Over that time, he has been able to introduce plants gradually and to compose a truly striking landscape. He straddles a

Little more than eighteen months after planting, the Native Plant Garden at the New York Botanical Garden, designed by Oehme, van Sweden, was impressively grown in. The central water feature filters storm water and creates additional habitats for a broad range of plants; the overall space is striking as well as educational.

line between ecological restoration and landscape design with the project, the remnant of an original prairie, and balances diversity with aesthetics. Increasing plant diversity over time allows a landscape to flower through a period of months to provide continuous color, again attracting visitors.

An institution created to entice the masses from the outset, the visitor center at the Brooklyn Botanic Garden in New York, designed by Weiss/Manfredi Architects and HMWhite, is surrounded by imaginative meadow plantings. The roof is planted with a tall-grass meadow, an unexpected feature for New York that attracts attention as soon as visitors approach and one that works well as a foil to the contemporary architecture. The metaphor of the wild coming to the city is immediately apparent. The tall grasses move in the wind and animate the structure throughout all four seasons. In addition, the plants manage storm water runoff from the structure and site.

At another city institution, the New York Botanical Garden, the renowned firm of Oehme, van Sweden demonstrates how a variety of ecologies can coexist on one 3.5-acre site. Their Native Plant Garden gives visitors a complete experience of the diversity of meadow plants found in the Northeastern United States. More than 100,000 individual plants were used to create an extraordinary variety of microclimates. The

ABOVE: The Native Plant Garden's topography rolls up and down; it hosts different moisture levels that in turn create a series of microclimates; Oehme van Sweden used this fact as an opportunity to incorporate a surprising number of individual ecologies.

RIGHT: *Carex plantaginea*, asters, maidenhair ferns, and other plants native to New York's woodland glades line a walk of pervious paving at the NYBG. The plants create strong contrasts between areas of sun and areas of shade, which keeps the eye dancing across the landscape and creates a feeling of comfortable seclusion.

LEFT: This rain garden at Cornell Plantations sets the benchmark for what is possible even with spaces that are usually considered waste areas. Wolf Landscape Architecture created a meadow of cloudlike *Panicum*, perennial sunflowers, and goldenrod and set it a next to a red maple–lined walk to greet visitors the moment they step out of their cars.

ABOVE: Blue flag iris, joe-pye weed, and crimson cardinal flowers inhabit and thrive in the moister areas of the site.

Larry Weaner seeded this meadow at Kosciuszko Park in Stamford, Connecticut. Forbs, rather than grasses, dominate the planting matrix. This creates a different type of meadow than is usually seen.

sun-soaked, broad, open areas are immersive and expressive, and shaded areas featuring subtly intermingled ferns and fall-blooming asters highlight an often-overlooked type of beauty. The firm also took advantage of the topography to create wet meadows adjacent to a central cascading pool—also a storm water management feature—and dry meadows in the upland areas. A deep understanding of plants and native flora converges with design skill here to craft a landscape that teaches by enticing visitors to stop and appreciate the painterly composition.

At Cornell Plantations in Ithaca, New York, Wolf Landscape Architecture designed a wet meadow intended to manage storm water runoff for a nontraditional space—a strip of land adjacent to a parking area. These wet meadows serve as bioretention and filtration gardens and also greet visitors with a dynamic, colorful, and engaging landscape that sets the tone for the rest of the garden experience. Rain gardens are now required in some municipalities, but all too often they end up looking like planted ditches. Here they become a design feature in their own right and show that with a

RIGHT: *Pycnanthemum* is an underused native plant. Its white bracts are striking in both meadows and more formal planting schemes. It contrasts pleasantly with little bluestem—turning red for autumn—and with drifts of butter and eggs in the midground.

thoughtful and intentional eye, even a parking lot can become an aesthetic asset and provide a memorable sense of arrival. Tall grasses and joe-pye weed, in particular, impress with their sheer scale. By late summer, the rain gardens have become lush, expressive features that build anticipation about a visit to the rest of the arboretum.

Larry Weaner, a landscape designer based just outside of Philadelphia, tends to seed his meadows rather than using more expensive plugs, though he does employ both methods. He has added a very diverse, seeded meadow to an existing residential garden that covers a hillside in North Salem, New York that capitalizes in particular on one of grasses' best advantages—their ability to catch light. Few other plants help a viewer appreciate just how dramatically light does change throughout the day. His other project featured here, Kosciuszko Park in Stamford, Connecticut, was also seeded. This approach is revealed in both gardens' ultimate aesthetic: when a diverse mix of native meadow species is directly seeded into the ground, it yields a less-composed and more ecological community of plants because the various species

germinate and grow on the site where they are best suited. Competition between species is a stronger component of the process, and it yields a different effect that is less intentional-looking, perhaps, but more diverse. These two projects appear to be more loosely composed than some of the other meadow gardens featured here simply because of the method of execution.

Established more than ten years ago, the dry mountain meadow at the Denver Botanic Gardens has recently come into its full potential thanks to the gardeners' skill and long-term commitment to its welfare. Botanical gardens have the advantage of being maintained by skilled staff who remain interested in increasing species diversity over time, and their efforts have yielded a phenomenally diverse ecology in suburban Denver. Meadows are more difficult to establish in climates that receive little rainfall and are very dry in summer. Plants adapted to these drier regions also grow more slowly than plants in wet Eastern states; excluding nonnative, invasive plants is the trick to success. Weeding is a higher priority and an absolute necessity to get a native meadow fully established. This is expensive, and takes a real commitment on the part of the client. Here, a basic matrix of plants was established to achieve cover, then was supplemented with seeding and small plants to add diversity.

ABOVE, LEFT: In this North Salem, New York, garden by Larry Weaner, the meadows extend the landscape beyond the formal gardens immediately adjacent to the home. Several design professionals have worked in collaboration with the owner, who is a highly accomplished gardener in her own right.

ABOVE: A variety of phloxes in white and lavender, which are often forgotten to be prairie natives, are used in conjunction with joe-pye weed to transition the formal garden into the naturalistic landscape.

A simple bench set in a small area of lawn invites a close-up contemplation of the meadows that extend around it on all sides.

Nelson Byrd Woltz is also an advocate of meadow planting, and the firm has introduced meadows in several of the private garden projects they have created. Their design for a residence in Connecticut, a 300-acre working farm, takes advantage of the site's scale and hillside topography by enhancing its vistas with meadow grasses that draw the eye toward horizon points and forests in the distance and embracing the property's unique qualities, such as large ledges of exposed granite, by surrounding

LEFT AND ABOVE: The high plains prairie at the Denver Botanic Gardens has been evolving for over a decade as Dan Johnson, its curator of native plants, has been adding diversity through plants and seed. The silver tones of the foliage in these drought-resistant plants, including the sparkly white-flowered *Erigeron divergens* and the towering, gold-flowered *Senecio spartioides* created a lovely frame for Dale Chihuly's *Red Reeds*, a temporary installation in the summer of 2014. The main grass is *Pascopyrum smithii. Yucca glauca,* sage, the sunny yellow flowers of *Helianthus petiolaris,* and the gray foliage of *Artemisia frigida* add variety.

them with groupings of plants placed in a rhythmic arrangement that echoes the craggy striations of the rock. This approach celebrates the local landscape while also reducing maintenance for the homeowners.

Bernard Trainor, a designer with a practice based in Northern California, has become extraordinarily adept at adapting the meadow approach to sites on the West Coast, and to arid conditions in particular. The interplay between architecture, landscape architecture, and site is integrated and inseparable; all orient views out over the Carmel Valley in his Halls Ridge project. Trainor uses mass plantings of grasses to give the landscape a unified texture, which in turn impart an enhanced sense of space. Few or almost no flowers distract the eye; instead, the plantings near the house

LEFT: A single accent clump of coneflowers is all that's required to invite the meadow to approach the house's formal garden in this Connecticut landscape by Thomas Woltz.

RIGHT: A carved-stone sink is a contemporary take on the traditional garden fountain. Surrounded by coneflowers and fronted by short grasses, it seems to be an almost natural extension of the nearby rock outcropping.

LEFT: A stone ledge, concrete walls, meadow plantings, and a formal garden adjacent to the house all converge at the entrance to the farm compound.

RIGHT: Garden walls and coneflowers make a clear boundary between the landscape near the house and the grassy meadows that roll down the hills and to the native forest beyond.

Bernard Trainor punctuated a type of "lawn" composed of low-growing *Koeleria macrantha* with the porcupine-like *Muhlenbergia dubia*, which gives a naturalistic feel to the garden surrounding a raised pool. California live oaks at the perimeter relate to the scale of the home and to the surrounding hillside canopy.

act as a foreground to an exquisitely framed distant view. In this way, the immediate landscape takes advantage of the larger landscape as well.

In all of these contemporary interpretations, the traditional definition of a meadow as a vast, untamed expanse untouched by human hands is adapted in a very intentional way. Gardens that are more densely planted than would occur in nature, that are arranged according to bloom schedules, or that are punctuated with occasional nonnative species for impact make the style a viable option for today's residential and institutional spaces while honoring the original ecology.

LEFT: Trainor creates a strong foreground for the view and a sense of negative and positive space simply by mixing three grasses. The burnished-orange *Sesleria* 'Greenlee' is the mid-height grass, which adds color to the composition of the larger *Muhlenbergia dubia* and the lower *Koeleria macrantha*.

RIGHT: Russell Page said there are two kinds of garden: those that focus in on themselves and those that help us look out onto the larger world. Here Trainor frames the view to the hills beyond with casually formed stone walls that evoke ruins, a pool that reflects the evening sky, and plants with soft forms that blend the immediate landscape into the larger setting.

Ecological

PLANTING APPROACHES

"Persistence and determination alone are omnipotent."

CALVIN COOLIDGE

Planting styles based on the idea that plants should be arranged by their native ecologies were first proposed by German and Dutch landscape designers, and arrived in America only after works by their early proponents were published in English. Karl Foerster (1874–1970) was one of the earliest to initiate and promote these concepts, which have had immeasurable influence on garden design ever since. His core goals were to reduce maintenance and management in finished gardens, to limit the need for applications of fertilizer, and to reduce excessive water usage. Ecological plantings are not always based on an exclusive use of native plants; more often, interest is added by grouping plants from the same ecologies but different countries or continents. An example of this would be combining moor grass from Eurasia, coneflowers from North America, and knotweed from Asia—all are meadow plants. The same approach can be applied to perennials, trees, shrubs, or bulbs. Plants from similar habitats simply require fewer resources to manage if placed in a garden setting that replicates their native environment. This all sounds logical in hindsight with our now-ingrained ecological sensitivites, but it was a revolutionary theory for its time.

PREVIOUS PAGES AND ABOVE: Karl Foerster's own garden in Germany reveals how the ecological planting style he pioneered can result in a romantic mix of plantings. A nurseryman with the heart of poet, he looked to nature for inspiration; he used more grasses than Gertrude Jekyll or William Robinson and strove to utilize plants in places and formations that resembled their native ecologies to reduce maintenance. He even bred his own delphinium for drought tolerance, smaller flowers, and durability by using the American *Delphinium exaltatum*, which is a prairie plant.

RIGHT: A border planted with daylilies, joe-pye weed, and euphorbias show how Foerster emphasized associating plants from the same ecological niches.

LEFT: The big, fluffy *Persicaria polymorpha* is not well known, but it is useful for adding scale to perennial plantings thanks to its towering, six-foot height. Begonias add a simplicity and visual pause to the mixed plantings in the rest of the garden.

RIGHT: *Salvia* and *Lythrum* leavened with daisies' contrasting flower forms make a satisfying composition within a framework of deciduous trees and shrubs.

A grid of fastigiate ginkgos give structure to the planting at the Art Institute of Chicago by Northwind Perennial Farm. The dominant grass is *Calamagrostis* x *acutiflora* 'Karl Foerster,' but there is also red-flowering *Euphorbia griffithii* in the foreground. Perennials are mixed, as in Foerster's own garden, though here the plants are arranged into large groups to suit the scale of the institutional space.

Richard Hansen and Friedrich Stahl wrote a very comprehensive book, *Perennials and Their Garden Habitats*, originally published in German in 1981, that includes dozens of site assessments and formulas for specific planting applications. It is a compendium of keen observation, clear illustrations, tables and lists of plants to be used together, and information on soil conditions, light, water regimens, and maintenance protocols. It is essentially a textbook filled with formulas for a modern planting style. Piet Oudolf has also published many books in English now, with Henk Gerritsen and

LEFT: A mass of *Calamintha nepeta* shows up prominently in the late-season garden at the Art Institute of Chicago. Here it is mixed with grasses, perennial alliums that flowered earlier in the season, and a few coneflowers.

RIGHT: *Coreopsis tripteris* is a little-known but excellent hardy perennial for the garden. Here it is used with Russian sage and *Calamagrostis* x *acutiflora* 'Karl Foerster,' a durable and visually striking cultivar.

ABOVE: Adam Woodruff combines *Echinacea purpurea* 'White Swan,' Russian sage, and *Calamagrostis* x *acutiflora* 'Karl Foerster' with white *Veronicastrum* for good measure and with the little-known *Silphium terebinthinaceum* at a garden in Illinois. The towering but sparse eight-foot flower spikes of the latter add an element of drama without being overwhelming.

OPPOSITE: The combination of *Salvia nemorosa* 'Mai Nacht' and moonshine yarrow create a compelling field of complementary colors.

Noel Kingsbury. Piet's own garden—and former nursery—Hummelo, which he runs with his wife, Anja, were the proving grounds for the development of his own interpretation of this style. His work has now become familiar to U.S. audiences due to his participation in Millennium Park, in Chicago, and on the High Line, in New York City. His books often include extensive plant lists, and their evocative images make them enticing and accessible. Roy Diblik expands on these ideas in *The Know Maintenance Perennial Gardening*, a title that is intended to be friendly for the North American home gardener. Cassian Schmidt, who is virtually unknown in the United States, teaches planting design and manages the Schau- und Sichtungsgarten Hermannshof in Weinheim, Germany, and is driving the style further. He publishes prolifically, gives away tested plant combinations to the trade, and defines maintenance regimes for his planting associations, but all in German so few are aware of his work in the English-speaking world— except in association with the popular fountain grass *Pennisetum alopecuroides* 'Cassian's Choice,' named by plantsman Kurt Bluemel to honor his friend.

CREATING PLANT COMMUNITIES

Matrix planting is related to ecological planting in that it often features a complex mix of species that replicates to some degree how native plant communities seed in the wild. Designers, however, make choices about color, texture, and form that reinterpret the natural look; this point of view reflects what nature teaches about

composition but distills it for impact. Matrix planting, as opposed to drift or mass planting, is becoming increasingly popular. Individual species plants are not used in continuous groups that are kept separate from one other, but are interspersed. Whole communities are built up in this manner and the communities gradually shift, creating very artistic landscapes. Layering is key; it maximizes each cubic foot of soil. Bulbs and ephemerals—plants that emerge and go dormant quickly, most common in woodland ecologies—are commingled in matrix schemes with longer-growing perennials and even woody plants.

Plant selection for ecologically minded gardens can be geographically wide-ranging; it need not be limited to a site's native plants. Today's cultural environmental consciousness sometimes tempts designers to try all-native plantings, but if a plant like blue flag (*Iris versicolor*), which requires a lot of water, is planted with a little bluestem or *Andropogon*, which are adapted to dryer soils, one will fail. While all are North American natives, they are not from the same ecologies. On the other hand, *Echinacea* grows wonderfully next to *Salvia nemorosa*, though they are from different continents.

LEFT: An area of Chanticleer's garden planted with Virginia cedars, little bluestem, and sunflowers in seed comes into its own in late autumn.

RIGHT: The Chanticleer gardening staff created a radical reinterpretation of a lawn. A charmingly shaggy and unkempt area of grass is interplanted with bulbs for spring perennials and the South African annual *Osteospermum* in crystalline white.

Steve Martino uses the vastly different forms of palo verde, *Agave weberi*, and opuntia to create an eye-catching border to a swimming pool. The planting masks a parking court while also providing a frame and foreground for the dramatic view of the mountains beyond.

It is useful to study naturally occurring plant communities in situ so that natural associations can be expanded upon and stylized in a garden setting. Another key component to the ecological style is choosing species that can age and go dormant without grooming, by leaving forms with inherent structural interest or seed heads, for example. This celebrates the whole life cycle of a plant and is in opposition to planting styles where staking, deadheading, and generally intensive efforts are spent manipulating plants for compositional and/or aesthetic reasons.

EXAMPLES FROM DIFFERENT ECOLOGIES

Ecological plantings that blend species from around the globe create an overall effect of many different plants growing happily together, yet relating to one other in some perceptible way chosen by the designer. That being said, many designers take liberty with the various components of this technique. Piet Oudolf often plants in fairly defined groupings, for example, which creates a composed-looking and emotionally impactful design; he usually limits his color palette to muted tones

RIGHT: *Pedilanthus macrocarpus* and Monstrose cactus frame a path that leads to a tall *Lophocereus schottii* and a garden wall with artfully exposed rebar that mimics the form of the succulent nearby.

LEFT: A richly varied composition of plants that thrive in arid conditions is given rhythm thanks to blue *Agave weberi* while a tuft of *Nolina nelsonii* in front of the purple wall punctuates the whole by acting as sculpture. The mixed planting makes even this desert setting feel refreshing.

Stongly vertical senita cactus and multibranched cardon cactus are interspersed
with mounds of silver-gray brittlebush (*Encelia farinosa*) by Colwell Shelor, providing physical separation and visual relief from the upright forms.

An encyclopedic collection of aloes arranged in masses by Colwell Shelor high-lights differences in size, growth habit, and variations in color at the entryway to this home. The tree-form *Aloe dichotoma* provides a strong focal point.

Candelabro cactus (*Pachycereus weberi*) create a Southwestern take on a traditional allée along this entry drive. They are underplanted with golden barrel cactus and the beautiful *Agave parryii*—which is hardy to zone 6 if planted in a free-draining soil.

to unite the whole. Roy Diblik, owner of Northwind Perennial Farm in Burlington, Wisconsin, has fused the matrix style and plant choices similar to Oudolf's into his own vocabulary that is painterly and sophisticated. His planting designs are inspired by the look and feel of the Midwest prairies. He is adept at mixing plants from around the world, often combining grasses and perennials in equal parts. He looks to his native landscape for a point of departure and his planting plans strongly reflect the region he works and gardens in, as can be seen at his garden for the Art Institute of Chicago.

Adam Woodruff, a designer from Clayton, Missouri, has been strongly influenced by Piet Oudolf. He is a rising designer from the younger generation, with a deep knowledge of plants and a flair for visually intriguing combinations that result in artfully naturalistic gardens that look at home in his own corner of the Midwest. He has much to contribute and a long career ahead.

The talented group of gardeners at Chanticleer, near Philadelphia, never stop experimenting and never fail to put their own spin on current trends. The project featured here, a lawn near the pool, is a perfect example. The closely shorn, traditional prototype was thrown out in favor of a charmingly shaggy replacement studded

LEFT: An elliptical water feature and a grouping of oblong terra-cotta pots add both permanent and movable accent features to this sitting area, which was surrounded with a wide selection of aloes by Colwell Shelor. Palo verde trees provide relief from the Arizona sun.

RIGHT: The strict geometry of a curving stone wall is at once tempered and accentuated by a variety of aloes, including the tree-form *Aloe ferox*.

ABOVE: James Corner Field Operations, with Greenlee and Associates, took the unusual and eye-catching step of underplanting deciduous trees with agaves as well as clump-forming grasses at Tongva Park.

RIGHT: The blue tones of *Agave attenuata* are accentuated when given a backdrop of cream-colored stucco walls.

ABOVE: Tall *Muhlenbergia lindheimeri* lining a set of stairs gives visitors to Tongva Park in Santa Monica, California, an intimate experience with the seed heads.

RIGHT: The arching, feathery flower spikes of *Pennisetum spathiolatum* are an effective counterpoint to the hardness of a stainless-steel fence; they also repeat the curved form of the facade to a tunnel's entry in the distance.

LEFT: *Morea* lining this fence will flower with the iris-like blooms for which it is famous early in summer; in early autumn, as seen here, its stalks create a unifying foil to the variety of grasses and agaves planted across the walkway.

BELOW: Field Operations and Greenlee and Associates planned for the monstrous flower spike of an *Agave attenuata* to arch above a field planted with other agaves and *Muhlenbergia rigens*, adding early autumn drama.

LEFT: Spiny acanthus, drumstick alliums, 'Rozanne' geraniums and 'Sapphire Blue' sea hollies are woven together to give a lush setting to a section of blue-and-turquoise glass sculptures at Chihuly Garden and Glass.

RIGHT: The hybrid dogwood 'Celestial' is underplanted here with *Geum* 'Totally Tangerine,' which blooms for a good two months in Seattle—and most of the rest of the country. It is a breakthrough in the genus and very worth using.

Drifts of Ramapo rhododendron precede the summer-flowering perennials in this bed.
To keep the garden appealing to visitors in every season, 45,000 bulbs were also layered
into the garden to provide flowers in February, starting with squills and early crocuses.

Mahonia japonica—hardy to -20F—is mixed with regal, lady, and Wallich's ferns to create a woodland setting for a section of the garden colonized with Chihuly's *Lavender Reeds*. These are underplanted with *Camassia leichtlinii* and hardy cyclamen that flower in winter. At least five progressions of flowers grace most areas of this intensely planted, three-quarter-acre garden.

The shaded area around the *Lavender Reeds* feels very lush in midsummer, as the wide variety of ferns that surrounds them grow into their fullest expression of the year.

with bulbs and self-sowing hardy annuals. The effect is imaginative and memorable. Elsewhere in the garden, they have mixed native cedars with little bluestem and backed them with the seed heads of sunflowers; they embrace innovative plant combinations and associations, much to the delight of visitors.

Ecological planting styles are perhaps even more useful and important for arid settings. Steve Martino, based in Phoenix, Arizona, has worked throughout the Southwest on projects that reflect this style, and which are based on his deep and direct experience with native desert flora. He relies heavily on native plants, but does not use them exclusively; he adds a softness to his projects by incorporating desert perennials and ephemerals with the stronger and more expected forms of various cactus. The final result is a mood of lushness in the desert, although this at first seems like an oxymoron. He also creates bold architectural statements both with plant material and with a fearless application of color to hardscape elements. His gardens are dynamic and invigorating, making them a welcome respite in hot climates.

Although the principals of Colwell Shelor both formerly worked in Steve Martino's office, they have achieved a distinctly different point of view. Their

LEFT: *Eryngium* 'Sapphire Blue,' with it steely, spiky flowers, draws a lot of attention from visitors. Here it is mixed with prostrate-growing yews, weeping Japanese maples, and the dependable geranium 'Rozanne,' which flowers from May through November.

RIGHT: Spring explodes in this section of the garden with hundreds of *Allium* 'Globemaster,' *Allium hollandicum* 'Purple Sensation,' and *Geranium* x *cantabrigiense* 'St. Ola.' The alliums repeat the spherical form of the floats and are a popular display when flowering. These two alliums are also very dependable perennial varieties.

designs feel deliberate and unified, and are often deep studies in a narrow range of form and texture. The project illustrated here does not at first seem like an ecological planting, but upon closer inspection the viewer realizes the various species are interplanted and arranged in drifts. They are also adept at the use of grasses that thrive in the desert. The range of plants they select for a project expresses a very definite feeling.

John Greenlee started his career as a nurseryman specializing in native and exotic grasses for the California market. He has long conducted trials to understand what could and would grow dependably in Northern and Southern California, and he has accordingly been tapped to design gardens based on his unique experience with grasses in their native habitats, including with James Corner Field Operations. His plantings are always very animated, because grasses move so much and change with the environment and the light. In his more recent projects, he is beginning to add structural plants to provide strong focal points including aloes and agaves; these also offer striking contrasts to the finely textured grasses when used in close proximity.

Land Morphology, our firm, made use of the ecological style of planting at Chihuly Garden and Glass in Seattle for one very practical reason: the garden is only

LEFT: A Sonoma dove tree, the shrubby–as opposed to vining–*Lonicera pileata*, and prostrate blue spruce form a simple backdrop to Chihuly's *Metallic Herons*. Sensual Touch tulips that must be replanted annually are included to add color for visitors early in the year.

RIGHT: Exuberant *Allium schubertii* and black-and-yellow striped violas are interplanted among ferns to provide flowers next to a black float and a black *Saguaro* glass piece in early spring.

RIGHT: Weathered-steel retaining walls suggest terraces; Ron Lutsko planted both native and exotic perennials around them that reference the native plants just beyond, on the knoll.

BELOW: The retaining walls become risers for the stairs at the entry of this home near Sun Valley, Idaho, designed by Allied Works Architecture. A mix of yarrow, grasses, penstemon, and alders provide a demure but sophisticated welcome.

three-quarters of an acre but receives in excess of half a million visitors a year, and perennials thrive in dense communities. The firm created a strong framework of woody plants to define and form space, but layered in thousands of flowering shrubs, perennials, and bulbs to cover every square foot of the garden, maximizing the limited planting area. In most areas of the garden, we achieved five to eight flowering cycles of various plants in the course of a season, ten in a few places. Due to the intense visitation numbers and the corresponding expectation that the garden will constantly be in bloom, the firm also planted violas, pansies, and ornamental cabbages and kales among the permanent plants for winter and early spring interest. It is a plant-dense garden, with flowers to view in every week of the year.

RIGHT: Strongly rectilinear concrete forms are softened by chokecherry and the bright *Penstemon eatonii*. A copse of cottonwood edges the composition at the garden's perimeter.

BELOW: Ron Lutsko used the durable and lovely moonshine yarrow along the entry steps; it is exceptionally hardy and dependable in cold, rugged mountain climates like those of Idaho, Montana, and Wyoming.

Emphasis was placed on using perennials because they have a longer flowering season than shrubs and bulbs. Careful selection of the flower colors has been considered to accentuate and visually support the glass art, either through complementary associations or contrasting colors. The art is fully integrated into the plantings; the combinations of organic and inorganic elements are very much intended to help them play off each other. Since many of the glass forms are derived from nature—saguaro cactus, eel grass, marlins, herons, snake heads and more—the resulting dialogue between forms is rich.

Ron Lutsko, who is based in San Francisco, has created ecological gardens based on native meadow plantings as well. This requires a base knowledge of various ecological systems, and both have taken on

This Northern California garden by Bernard Trainor is a mix of plant types, but all share the common trait of being drought tolerant. There is no irrigation system in this garden, a testament to the designer's understanding of the various ecologies of the plants used.

Bronze-leaved New Zealand flax is planted between the rosettes of *Echeveria* and *Aeonium*, creating a striking juxtaposition of geometry along a narrow strip of land between a swimming pool and stucco garden wall.

residential projects sited on mountain slopes that use the surrounding low, native vegetation as inspiration. Ketchum, near Sun Valley in Idaho, is a harsh climate to garden in. The summers are scorchingly hot and the winters bitterly cold, so any plants Lutsko selected for cold hardiness also needed to be adapted to dry summers. He relies on lower-growing vegetation from dry prairies, and the design of the garden also feels a little more crafted and intense than the surrounding landscape, which announces to visitors that they are not in a wild landscape, but rather just on the edge of it.

For a residence in Palo Alto, California, Bernard Trainor amassed an absolute copia of succulents, many of which relate to the vibrant aqua of a nearby swimming pool. The result is a real lesson in what can be achieved with this plant family in terms of color and texture.

Moving back to the temperate zone, the Blume project designed by our firm, Land Morphology, was based on a request from the client for a naturalistic garden that would soften an otherwise formal landscape and create a strong and romantic foreground to the view of Lake Washington available from the house. All plants used are meadow species, but since the desired effect wasn't for an actual meadow, a mix of native and nonnative species was selected. A heavy emphasis was placed on forbs and

LEFT: At this residence on Lake Washington next to Seattle, Land Morphology replaced a former lawn with a variety of perennials and a handful of woody plants such as *Rosa glauca* to create a more eco-logical and interesting transition from the formal garden next to the house and the rest of the property. Nepetas and knotweed are used here with phlox, coneflowers, Spanish oats, and 'Skyracer' moor grass. This meadow-like planting provides color long into the growing season thanks to the long-flowering *Persicaria amplexicaulis* 'Atrosanguinea.'

RIGHT: Waves of perennials in pink, white, lavender, and crimson create an informal frame for the view from the house's formal gardens down to Lake Washington. Cut sandstone stairs and a gravel walk link the mixed meadow to the formal land-scape closer to the home.

summer- and autumn-flowering plants. Plugs helped the area to mature quickly and now that it is established, it requires less maintenance than the lawn that was in the space previously—and it's far more interesting to look at.

In Lousiana, Jeffrey Carbo combines a modern framework with deft planting design adapted to extremely humid summer heat. He, like many designers represented here, is adept at moving between several planting styles and at selecting the most appropriate for the project at hand. A modernist at heart, his strong, rational, and well-detailed built forms are paired with complex plantings that feel welcoming and intimate. He is adept at combining trees, shrubs, perennials, and grasses to create immediately recognizable associations or, equally, in displaying plants in a sparer and more sculptural way. Shade is important in the South, so trees are often grouped into bosques and underplanted with diverse collections of ferns, sedges, and grasses to create woodlands that are, above all, refreshing.

ENVIRONMENTAL STEWARDSHIP MEETS SHEER BEAUTY

What Karl Foerster pioneered in Germany in the mid-twentieth century is here to stay. As garden design moves toward celebrating plants first and built forms second, and as awareness of the necessity of environmental stewardship continues to seat itself deep in the collective cultural psyche, the ecological planting style begins to look increasingly compelling. This style of planting allows designers to explore the diverse plant offerings today's global connectivity provides while helping to conserve resources for tomorrow. Environmental considerations are the single biggest driver causing professional landscape architects and designers to learn more about new plants again and to develop new and inspiring ways of using them, and the gardens are benefiting. As an appreciation for design in general has spread to the masses, the demand for well-crafted and intriguingly detailed gardens—public and private—has increased. Plants used in an attractive way can make people celebrate local ecology, leading to increased curiosity about the environment as a whole and perpetuating the cycle of good environmental governance.

OPPOSITE: A plank bridge delves through a copse of river birches and a mixed ground cover of wood ferns and Louisiana iris, linking two lawns in this garden by Jeffrey Carbo. The loose woodland plantings seem all the more lush thanks to the crisp stone retaining walls.

'Allee' elms and *Magnolia grandiflora* 'Claudia Wannamaker' build up to an expanse of loblolly pines, creating an interface with the lawn and Louisiana forest in this garden by Jeffrey Carbo. The introduction of plants appropriate to the edge of a woodland bestow the property with an authentic feeling, albeit in a highly structured form.

River rocks line the center of a rain garden, strengthening the sight line through a geometrically planted grove of river birch. By simply turning one plank in the bridge perpendicular to the others, Jeffrey Carbo strengthens the entire design.

SEASONAL AND TEMPORARY Plantings

"The true gardener must be brutal—and imaginative for the future."

VITA SACKVILLE-WEST

Annuals, tender perennials, and temporary plantings are all used as ways of enlivening space. People love color and plants with color make architecture and urban spaces more humane: it's that simple. We crave some expression of nature wherever we are, but permanent plantings are not always suitable for every space due to limited open land or adverse growing conditions. Municipalities and commercial real-estate managers are increasingly coming to view plants as assets that will invite and encourage people to use their spaces. They see the value in adding planters to plazas, street medians, and entries to buildings. In private residences, containers can be focal points that enhance the lines of the architecture or enliven a porch or entryway, increasing curb appeal. Gardens are becoming highly valued; the fact that the land adjacent to the High Line on the west side of Manhattan has exploded with new development since that park opened is the best example of this trend. A garden can be expressed creatively with changeable and temporary plantings, making them just as important a category of design to explore as full landscapes.

VICTORIAN CONTRIBUTIONS

It was during the Victorian Era that the inclusion of annuals—or, more accurately, tender perennials—in gardens became prevalent. Most plants used in annual beds are actually perennials that are simply not hardy in temperate climates. The ornate conservatories of the period were developed in part to help these grow and propagate; with the Industrial Revolution came steel that could be forged in large pieces and glass that could be manufactured in large sheets to create the fancifully shaped greenhouses that are some of the era's most enduring monuments. Joseph Paxton, an engineer and horticulturist who was employed at Chatsworth, in England, built the first of these, nicknamed "the Great Stove" for its shape. With it, Paxton started a craze for conservatories on private estates; these features used specialized horticulture as a display of wealth.

Global travel became faster during the same period, and tropical plants were increasingly imported to America and Europe from far-off lands. Coleus, for example, was first introduced into England in the late-nineteenth century from Malaysia and Southeast Asia.

RIGHT: Variegated tapioca is an annual worth seeking out; its palmate leaves with a yellow flare in the center and red petioles give it an unusual depth.

BELOW: Containers are useful for changing plantings from season to season in a manageable way. Here variegated *Plectranthus* and an orange begonia adorn a path at Chanticleer.

Its proliferation perhaps epitomizes the Victorians' love of tropical plants and tender perennials. Coleus 'Pineapple Beauty' was one of the original five selected in the late 1880s, and it is still widely available today. The wealthy and middle classes were fascinated by such "exotic" species, and the gentry built private conservatories to hold them and/or employed legions of gardeners to design and plant elaborate summer bedding schemes to display them. The middle classes could also enjoy carefully planned displays of newly introduced species in public parks and botanical gardens. Institutional plantings were elaborate and often laid out in geometric patterns such as ribbons, whence the term "carpet bedding."

The era's two most famous gardeners felt differently about including annuals in gardens, interestingly enough. Gertrude Jekyll used tender perennials including dahlias and scarlet sage in her famous long border at Munstead Wood, her home in Surrey, England. The last chapter of her famous *Colour Schemes for the Flower Garden* features a description of a garden room there where she mixed hardy and tender plants together for a summer-long show of flowers and color. This idea resurfaced in England and America at the end of the twentieth century when garden

LEFT: These colorful tropical plantings belie the fact that this garden is in North-Central New Jersey. In the Hardie garden, Land Morphology created a fantastical 40-foot-square garden with coleus, red angelwing begonias, tropical fig trees in two colors, and variegated euonymus for structure.

ABOVE: Visually tempting but very prickly *Solanum pyracanthum* features dangerous orange thorns. Its fuzzy gray leaves contrast in a very graphic way with wine- and plum-colored coleus.

writer Ann Lovejoy renamed the style "tropicalismo." What goes around comes around! William Robinson, however, reacted strongly to what he deemed annual-heavy, "artificial" planting schemes; he of course went on to favor less formal and more "wild-looking" planting ideas. Robinson was mostly opposed to a structured, patterned use of tender plants—not to using them at all—but he did also advocate for bringing native plants found in regional landscapes into cottage gardens.

MODERNIST INTERPRETATIONS

As the modernists peeled away ornamental details in architecture as well as landscape architecture, elaborate, temporary horticulture designs gradually fell out of favor. They were seen as being "less serious" than permanent schemes since any given design was necessarily transient. It is refreshing to see all types of plants being embraced again and coming back into favor with landscape and garden designers of both public and private places; the value color and immediate seasonal interest can provide to a space cannot be overstated.

Roberto Burle Marx influenced this style of planting as well. Of course, as a Brazilian landscape architect, he was using the tender perennials we recognize as annuals in the United States where they appear as perennials—and therefore creating permanent plantings. When his bold, colorful projects began to be published internationally in the 1960s and 1970s, however, his taste influenced how stylish designers brought high-impact and modern interpretations to temporary plantings in temperate climates. His influence is still recognizable today in the big swaths of petunias, coleus, and similarly colorful plants often found at the entrances to commercial office parks, malls, and housing developments. Thomas Church, who initially designed bean-shaped beds to complement his iconic kidney-bean shaped swimming pool at the Donnell Garden in Sonoma, California, has also been endlessly reinterpreted.

ABOVE: Light catches the trellis and arbor in the Herb Garden at the Brooklyn Botanic Garden. Sweetly scented valerian waves in the foreground.

RIGHT: Almost all vegetables are annuals or tender perennials, so they are rarely used in graphic planting schemes. The Herb Garden at the Brooklyn Botanic Garden, however, includes many food crops used in a patterned way. These are changed seasonally. Caleb Leech, the curator, creates amazing plant combinations that obviate the desire for showy flowers in this part of the garden.

Celosia and rainbow chard provide a display
of pure, primary colors all summer long at the
Brooklyn Botanic Garden.

ADVANTAGES OF TENDER PERENNIALS

There are many valid and practical reasons for using tender perennials in a garden. They grow rapidly, attaining an impressive/wanted size quickly. They have extended flowering seasons as compared to temperate plants, and they come in absolutely brilliant colors. All of these attributes have maintained annuals' popularity over the last 150 years. Annuals are also immensely popular for container gardens, particularly as focal points. Larger displays have also stayed in vogue since the Victorians first popularized glass-house plants, and whole businesses thrive on performing seasonal display gardening services for private, public, and commercial places. In the 1800s, most annual plants were propagated by cuttings. Today propagation methods are from seed and micropropagation or tissue culture. The perception that annual bedding is expensive is true on one level, because the plants must be replaced annually, but given their high impact on a cost-per-square-foot basis, tender plants have a value in yielding sheer flower power that temperate plants simply cannot match.

In the temperate zones of the U.S., the appearance of plants with large foliage and bright colors impresses due to sheer scale and the cachet of exotic and far-off lands. Cannas, bananas, and elephant ears are popular large-leaved plants. Tender grasses, dahlias, and cordylines are also used extensively. Any distinctive color, form, or texture

Parsley, oakleaf lettuces, and kale are used to create a modern parterre in the Herb Garden. The display will last all summer long and well into the autumn, revealing one way annuals and tender perennials can be used in a planting scheme that endures for several months at a time.

can be achieved with tender perennials—including a full range of designs from subtle to garish. Elephant's ears *Alocasia* and *Colocasia*, for example, are easy to produce and always eye-catching. By contrast, in milder climates like the Deep South and California, "winter" displays that showcase specimens that will not tolerate summertime in those zones can appear as striking to residents as tropical plantings do in the rest of the country the rest of the time. Plants that tolerate cool temperatures, for example, like snapdragons, pansies, violas, and cyclamen, can stand in for those that like it hot and humid, such as impatiens and salvias.

Clients who own large estates also often appreciate—and expect to include—highly designed bedding schemes and container plantings as part of the larger landscape. At Land Morphology, we design summer planting schemes in January and winter schemes in June and July. Since the marketplace contains many different growers of bedding plants and varieties are constantly changing, it takes a knowledge of the marketplace and diligence to keep up with trends and to be able to source plants for plans that have

an intensive design. Offering temporary display design services also gives landscape designers the opportunity to stay in front of their clients on a regular basis—an effective business development strategy.

We add tropical plants annually for sheer drama and impact to Graeme Hardie's garden in Nutley, New Jersey, for example. Over the past twenty years, seasonal plantings have been created that reference both his South African heritage and his exuberant and joyful demeanor. The section of the garden where we do this is framed by the house's cobalt blue walls and is barely 40 feet square. The garden is planted with more than 80 percent temperate perennials and woody plants overall, but the extensive use of containers on the terraces and the tender plants mixed into the beds in one area near the house give it the impression of a tropical retreat. It's just something different for the owner to experience.

INSTITUTIONAL AND CIVIC ADAPTATIONS

Marco Polo Stufano—a former director of horticulture at Wave Hill in New York City who influenced an entire generation of professional gardeners during his 34-year tenure there—was a contemporary torchbearer for the use of tender perennials in both containers and bedding schemes. For years, the refined horticulture happening at Wave Hill was considered the gold standard for public horticulture due to his sophisticated use of plants and the incredible variety of common and rare plant varieties he planted both in the ground and in containers. Each year at Wave Hill, one kidney-bean-shaped bed is always filled with flowering tropical plants as an exuberant celebration of summer. This particular bed is often is bolder in pattern than the rest of the Robinsonian-style garden; it is planted as an effective counterpoint to the rest of the landscape and visitors flock to it.

Botanical and public gardens have known for decades that changes in seasonal plantings will entice paying visitors to return again and again. The constituents' expectation for variety in plant collections must be met. It would take a prohibitive amount of money and effort to change permanent plants out annually. However, it is possible to change containers and areas of beds devoted to temporary plantings

Hoerr Schaudt designs the median planters that grace Michigan Avenue in Chicago. Castor beans, hot pink petunias, silver *Plectranthus*, milkweed, zinnias, and other unexpected species create an energized atmosphere for this premier tourism-and-shopping district.

radically from season to season and year to year. Longwood Gardens, near Kennett Square, Pennsylvania, attracts a million visitors a year; December, perhaps surprisingly, is its peak season because the garden creates staggeringly immense displays of tropical poinsettias in the impressive main conservatory building, in combination with other bedding plants. This always-thoughtful design forms a pleasant refuge from the often-harsh winter temperatures outside. These displays are not botanical collections per se, but massive seasonal landscape displays under glass.

The Longwood entry plaza features a new color scheme for each season for the same reason. The late summer/early autumn scheme illustrated here demonstrates the exuberant and engaging welcome its staff creates for visitors. This is as much about the perception of value for ticket price as it is about encouraging repeat visitation, but the point is that these annual and temporary plantings help Longwood fund itself to continue its larger mission.

Chanticleer in Wayne, Pennsylvania, is a pleasure garden that uses tender plants in highly imaginative ways. Container plantings feature prominently throughout the garden, often as monumental hanging baskets or wall plantings. This public garden

ABOVE: A detail of a Michigan Avenue planter, featuring orange zinnias, yellow-leaved sweet potato, purple *Cordyline*, and castor beans. This exuberant and lively combination of plants reads well from a distance—or through the window of a car.

RIGHT: Crate & Barrel has retained Hoerr Schaudt for over a decade to create plantings in front of its flagship store.

follows the basic tenets of Robinson and Jekyll: they mix tender perennials in with the larger garden's temperate plants in a naturalistic and romantic way.

Most vegetables are true annuals or tender perennials, so they are not often used as part of a graphic planting design within a garden. Plants in the Herb Garden at the Brooklyn Botanic Garden, however, are used in a dynamic and modern way as part of the display. Within the architectural and structural frame of the garden, the gardeners create ever-changing patterns of culinary, medicinal, dye, and flowering plants. This results in a rich and enveloping experience that both delights and informs visitors. Purple cabbages draw attention to themselves and their neighbors in a dramatic way when mixed with lavender-striped petunias and smoky purple-leaved sugarcane, for example! This new garden has quickly become one of the more popular destinations within the larger botanical garden.

Municipalities are increasingly learning to invest in tropical or annual plantings as a tool for economic development. Many tropical plants have a large scale that suits city surroundings, they can add intense color to gray or neutral concrete-and-stone streetscapes, and their lushness conveys a sense that a place is well cared for, safe,

ABOVE: *Alocasia* 'Calidora' is monumental in scale. It is mixed here with Persian shield, Begonia 'Dragon Wing Pink,' and lime sweet potato vine—quite the tropical explosion for the drop-off at O'Hare Airport!

RIGHT: Planters create a refreshing tropical welcome in summer and act as passive security buffers as well.

On Market Street in St. Louis, elephant ears, pink begonias, and fountain grass activate the business district and greet tourists to the city coming to see the green spaces near the state capitol.

and lively. More than fifteen years ago, Douglas Hoerr was commissioned to upgrade the planters in center of Michigan Avenue, in the heart of Chicago's retail district. Interestingly, individual property owners soon followed suit, adding plantings to their sidewalks and storefronts. The resulting effect is of a garden growing in the urban core of the third-largest city in America. The district is a dynamic place where people want to linger, live, and shop. Seasonal plantings also now greet arrivals at Chicago's O'Hare Airport—their heavy concrete bases also pragmatically serve as a low-grade security measure against errant vehicles.

In St. Louis, giant concrete planters overflowing with a mix of impressive species have been placed down the center median of the street leading up to the Missouri state capitol building. Manhattan has followed suit by funding in-ground displays of annuals planted in containers in Times Square. Local business taxing districts pay for most of this. Commercial clients also recognize the value of dressing up their commercial, residential, and retail properties in order to compete for tenants, to realize higher rents, and to increase their overall curb appeal. Rockefeller Center, for example, retains full-time, in-house staff to tend to its displays. In competitive real estate markets, an investment in seasonal, temporary plants is known to directly affect rents.

Engaging people with joyful plantings in bright colors and with bold foliage is simply good for business. Consequently, the range of plants now available for temporary displays can best be described as mind-boggling. A Ball Horticultural catalog or a visit to the botanical trial gardens in Chicago gives a small idea of just how many tropical plants are currently being propagated.

In Seattle, some of the best public horticulture in the city can be experienced at University Village—an outdoor shopping mall! Retail strategists fly in from all over the United States to see the designs on display and how they are executed for the commercial environment. The full range of horticultural delights can be encountered there, from bedding plants to hanging baskets and elaborate containers at every store's entrance. This approach helps the bottom line by attracting shoppers and national brands. Color and dynamic seasonal plantings relate to sales in very tangible ways, and therefore, display design is being taken ever more seriously by landscape design professionals.

LEFT: Variegated Moses-in-the-cradle is combined with spilling *Scaevola* by Adam Woodruff to create a commercial planter for the Laclede Center in Clayton, Missouri, that looks anything but expected.

ABOVE: The copper coleus in the center of this planter is known as Alabama Sunset, Texas Parking Lot, and a host of other names. It is a fast-growing and dependable variety that has recently reappeared in commerce. It used here with *Tradescantia*, zinnias, and Mexican feather grass.

FURTHER READING

GENERAL REFERENCES

Conran, Terence, and Dan Pearson. *The Essential Garden Book: Getting Back to Basics.* New York: Clarkson Potter, 1998.

Dirr, Michael A. *Dirr's Encyclopedia of Trees and Shrubs.* Portland, OR: Timber Press, 2011.

Dirr, Michael A. *Manual of Woody Landscape Plants: Their Identification, Ornamental Characteristics, Culture, Propogation and Uses.* Champaign, IL: Stipes Publishing, 2009.

Elliott, Brent. *The Country House Garden: From the Archives of Country Life: 1897–1939.* London: Mitchell Beazley, 1995.

Frieze, Charlotte M. *Private Paradise: Contemporary American Gardens.* New York: The Monacelli Press, 2011.

Harpur, Jerry. *Gardens in Perspective: Garden Design in Our Time.* London: Mitchell Beazley, 2007.

Phaidon Press, ed. *The Garden Book.* London: Phaidon, 2000.

Richardson, Tim, and Andrew Lawson. *The New English Garden.* London: Frances Lincoln, 2013.

Tankard, Judith B., and Michael Van Valkenburgh. *Gertrude Jekyll: A Vision of Garden and Wood.* New York: Abrams/Sagapress, 1990.

Taylor, Patrick, ed. *The Oxford Companion to the Garden.* New York: Oxford University Press, 2006.

Thomas, Graham Stuart. *The Art of Planting.* London: J. M. Dent, 1984

Thomas, Graham Stuart. *Ornamental Shrubs, Climbers and Bamboos.* London: Frances Lincoln, 2004.

Wilson, Andrew. *Influential Gardeners: The Designers Who Shaped 20th-Century Garden Style.* New York: Clarkson Potter, 2003.

PLANTS AS ARCHITECTURE

Bradley-Hole, Christopher. *The Minimalist Garden.* New York: The Monacelli Press, 1999.

Compton, Tania, Roger Malbert, and Marco Valdivia. *The Wirtz Private Garden.* B.A.I., 2009.

Farrand, Beatrix, and Diane Kostial McGuire. *Beatrix Farrand's Plant Book for Dumbarton Oaks.* Washington, D.C.: Dumbarton Oaks, 1980.

Hicks, David. *My Kind of Garden.* Woodbridge, Suffolk: Antique Collectors Club, 1999.

ARTFULLY NATURALISTIC GARDENS

Chatto, Beth. *The Damp Garden.* New York: Sagapress, Inc., 1996.

Chatto, Beth. *The Dry Garden.* New York: Sagapress, Inc., 1996.

Jekyll, Gertrude. *Colour Schemes for the Flower Garden.* Salem, NH: The Ayer Company, 1983.

Kameon, Judy. *Gardens Are for Living: Design Inspiration for Outdoor Spaces.* New York: Rizzoli, 2014.

Lord, Tony. *Gardening at Sissinghurst.* London: Frances Lincoln, 1995.

Ogden, Scott, and Lauren Springer Ogden. *Plant-Driven Design: Creating Gardens That Honor Plants, Place, and Spirit*. Portland, OR: Timber Press, 2008.

Robinson, William. *The English Flower Garden*. New York: Sagapress, 1989.

Robinson, William. *The Wild Garden*. Portland, OR: Timber Press, 2009.

Wilder, Louise Beebe. *Color in My Garden: An American Gardener's Palette*. New York: Atlantic Monthly Press, 1990.

GRAPHIC PLANTING DESIGN

Eliovson, Sima. *The Gardens of Roberto Burle Marx*. Portland, OR: Timber Press, 2003.

Jungles, Raymond. *The Colors of Nature: Subtropical Gardens by Raymond Jungles*. New York: The Monacelli Press, 2008.

Silva, Roberto. *New Brazilian Gardens: The Legacy of Burle Marx*. London: Thames & Hudson, 2014.

MEADOW GARDENS

Greenlee, John, and Saxon Holt. *The American Meadow Garden: Creating a Natural Alternative to the Traditional Lawn*. Portland, OR: Timber Press, 2009.

Jensen, Jens. *Siftings*. Baltimore, MD: Johns Hopkins University Press, 1990.

Lloyd, Christopher, Erica Hunningher, and Jonathan Buckley. *Meadows*. Portland, OR: Timber Press, 2004.

Steiner, Lynn M. *Prairie-Style Gardens: Capturing the Essence of the American Prairie Wherever You Live*. Portland, OR: Timber Press, 2010.

ECOLOGICAL PLANTING APPROACHES

Brookes, John. *John Brookes' Natural Landscapes*. New York: DK Publishing, Inc., 1998

Hansen, Richard, and Friedrich Stahl. *Perennials and Their Garden Habitats*. Portland, OR: Timber Press, 1993.

Kingsbury, Noel. *Gardening with Perennials: Lessons from Chicago's Lurie Garden*. Chicago: University of Chicago Press, 2014.

SEASONAL AND TEMPORARY PLANTINGS

Cooke, Ian. *The Plantfinder's Guide to Tender Perennials*. Newton Abbot, Devon, UK: David & Charles Publishers, 1998.

Joyce, David. *Readers Digest: The Complete Container Garden*. London: Frances Lincoln, 1996.

Roth, Susan A., and Dennis Schrader. *Hot Plants for Cool Climates: Gardening with Tropical Plants in Temperate Zones*. Portland, OR: Timber Press, 2005.

Thomas, Graham Stuart. *Perennial Garden Plants or the Modern Florilegium*. Portland, OR: Sagapress/Timber Press, 1990.

RESOURCES

WEST COAST

Amazing Maples
Japanese maples
Everett, Washington
amazingmaples.net

Bamboo Gardens
bamboo
North Plains, Oregon
bamboogarden.com

Bamboo Valley
bamboo
Albany, Oregon
bamboovalley.com

Blooming Nursery
flowering shrubs, ground covers, herbs, ornamental grasses, perennials
Cornelius, Oregon
bloomingnursery.com

Bluestem Nursery
grasses, willows
Laurier, Washington
bluestem.ca

Boxwood Farm
boxwoods
Mount Vernon, Washington
360-424-7423

Briggs Nursery
perennials
Elma, Washington
briggsnursery.com

Briggs Trees
perennials, shrubs, trees
Vista, California
briggstree.com

Buchholz & Buchholz Nursery
rare and specimen plants
Gaston, Oregon
buchholznursery.com

Cascade Tropicals
greenhouse plants, tropicals
Snohomish, Washington
206-623-9549

Clinton Bamboo
bamboo, tropicals
Seattle, Washington
clintonbamboo.com

D&M Nursery
large shrubs, topiaries
Canby, Oregon
dmnursery.com

Digging Dog Nursery
hard-to-find perennials, ornamental grasses, shrubs, trees, and vines
Albion, California
diggingdog.com

Don Schmidt Nursery
specimen Japanese maples
Boring, Oregon
donschmidtnursery.com

Edelweiss Perennials
specialty perennials
Canby, Oregon
edelweissperennials.com

Evergreen Nursery
perennials, shrubs
Oceanside, El Cajon, and San Diego, California
evergreennursery.com

Far Reaches Farm
mail order, rare plant specialist
Port Townsend, Washington
farreachesfarm.com

Forestfarm at Pacifica
bamboo, grasses, perennials, shrubs, trees
Williams, Oregon
forestfarm.com

Furney's Nursery
perennials, shrubs
Des Moines, Washington
furneysnursery.com

Gossler Farms
daphnes, epimediums, ferns, rhododendrons, shrubs
Springfield, Oregon
gosslerfarms.com

Griswold Nursery
azaleas, rhododendrons
Kirkland, Washington
griswoldnursery.com

Heritage Seedlings
rare deciduous ornamental trees and shrubs
Salem, Oregon
heritageseedlings.com

Iseli Nursery
dwarf conifers, Japanese maples, ornamental trees and shrubs
Boring, Oregon
iselinursery.com

Joy Creek Nursery
mail-order clematis, fuchsia, hosta, hydrangea, penstemon
Scappoose, Oregon
joycreek.com

Keeping It Green Nursery
mayapples, orchids, woodland perennials
Stanwood, Washington
keepingitgreennursery.com

L&B Nurseries
palms, subtropicals
Seattle, Washington
lb-nurseries.com

Naylor Creek Hosta Nursery
hostas and shade plants
Chimacum, Washington
naylorcreek.com

Northern Pacific Farm
cut stems, cut flowers
Canby, Oregon
northernpacificfarm.com

Northwest Garden Nursery
hellebores, podophyllums
Eugene, Oregon
northwestgardennursery.com

Northwest Nurseries
perennials, shrubs, trees
Redmond, Washington
nwnurseries.com

Northwest Wholesale Florist
floral wholesaler
Seattle, Washington
nwwholesaleflorists.com

Old Goat Farm
specialty nursery
Graham, Washington
oldgoatfarm.com

Plantmad Nursery
rare and difficult-to-propagate hardy ornamentals
Boring, Oregon
meacham.org/plantmad

Plants Northwest
perennials, shrubs, trees
Redmond, Washington
plantsnorthwest.net

Provitro Biosciences
bamboos
Mount Vernon, Washington
booshoot.com

San Marcos Growers
California native plants, ferns, ornamental grasses, perennials, trees, shrubs, succulents, vines
Santa Barbara, California
smgrowers.com

Schreiner's Iris Gardens
iris rhizomes
Salem, Oregon
schreinersgardens.com

Skagit Gardens
annuals and perennials
Mount Vernon, Washington
skagitgardens.com

Sundquist Nursery
epimediums, ferns, hostas, ornamental grasses, perennials for brighter locations, shade garden companions, woody plants
Poulsbo, Washington
sqnursery.com

T&L Nursery
grasses, ground covers, heathers, perennials, vines
Redmond, Washington
tandlnursery.com

Vibrant Plants
perennials, shrubs, trees
Woodinville, Washington
vibrantplants.com

Village Nurseries
perennials, shrubs, trees
Orange, California
villagenurseries.com

Weeks Roses
bare-root roses
Wasco, California
weeksroses.com

Wells Medina
annuals, azaleas, perennials, rhododendrons, shrubs, trees
Medina, Washington
wellsmedinanursery.com

Western Nursery Sales
shrubs, trees
Arlington, Washington
westernnurserysales.com

Whitman Farms
rare trees, shrub liners
Salem, Oregon
whitmanfarms.com

Wiggin's Nursery Company
specimen conifers, trees
Mount Vernon, Washington
wigginsnursery.com

ROCKY MOUNTAINS

Cashman Nursery
evergreens, fruit trees, ornamentals, shade trees, shrubs, vines
Bozeman, Montana
cashmannursery.com

Native Landscapes and Reclamation
natives, ornamentals
Livingston, Montana
nativelandscapes.wix.com

Westscape Wholesale
Nursery
adapted plants, natives
Belgrade, Montana
westscapenursery.net

MIDWEST

Arrowhead Alpines
*rare and unusual perennials,
woodland wildflowers, ferns,
alpines, dwarf conifers,
shrubs, trees*
Fowlerville, Michigan
arrowheadalpines.com

Bluebird Nursery, Inc.
mail-order specialty
Clarkson, Nebraska
bluebirdnursery.com

Klehm's Song Sparrow
*mail-order clematis, day-
lilies, hosta, peonies, perennials, woody plants*
Avalon, Wisconsin
songsparrow.com

Spring Meadow Nursery
*branched potted liners,
flowering shrub liners, shrubs*
Grand Haven, Michigan
springmeadownursery.com

Walter's Gardens/
Perennial Resource
grasses, perennials, plugs
Zeeland, Michigan
perennialresource.com

EAST COAST

Amherst Nurseries
shade trees
Amherst, Massachusetts
amherstnurseries.com

Bigelow Nurseries
conifers, shade trees
Northboro, Massachusetts
bigelownurseries.com

Blue Sterling Nursery
dwarf conifers
Bridgeton, New Jersey
bluesterling.com

Boltz Tree Farm & Nursery
conifers, trees
Fredericksburg, Pennsylvania
boltztreefarm.com

Brent and Becky's Bulbs
bulbs, perennials, seeds
Gloucester, Virginia
brentandbeckysbulbs.com

Classic Groundcovers
*annuals, grasses, ground
covers, hostas*
Athens, Georgia
classic-groundcovers.com

David's Nursery
*pot-in-pot grown woody
plants*
Exmore, Virginia
davidsnursery.com

East Coast Nurseries
grasses, shrubs, perennials
Riverhead, Long Island
eastcoastnurseries.com

Eaton Farms
container trees and shrubs
Leesport, Pennsylvania
eatonfarms.com

Flamingo Road Nursery
*ground covers, hedges, palms,
shade plants, trees, tropicals*
Davie, Florida
flamingoroadnursery.com

Flowerland Growers
annuals
Belvidere, New Jersey
908.475.2288

Galloway Farm Nursery
*bonsai, orchids, tropicals,
water lilies*
Miami, Florida
gallowayfarm.com

Garden Vision Epimediums
epimediums
Templeton, Massachusetts
epimediums.com

Gardino Nursery
rare and unusual plants
Delray Beach, Florida
rareflora.com

Halka Nurseries
specimen trees
Millstone, New Jersey
halkanursery.com

Wm. F. Hammell Nurseries
large trees
Honey Brook, Pennsylvania
hammellnurseries.com

Hoffman Nursery
*native and ornamental
grasses*
Rougemont, North Carolina
hoffmannursery.com

J.C. Hill Tree Farms
evergreen and shade trees
Orwigsburg, Pennsylvania
jchilltreefarms.com

Jesse Durko Tropical Garden
and Nursery
*flowering shrubs, orchids,
palms*
Davie, Florida
jessedurko.com

Juniper Hill Greenhouses
annuals, ground covers, herbs
Mattituck, New York
juniperhillgreenhouses.com

Kelly Wholesale Nurseries
fruit trees
Phelps, New York
kellywsn.com

Kurt Bluemel, Inc.
*bamboo, ferns, grasses,
perennials*
Baldwin, Maryland
kurtbluemel.com

Landcraft Environments
*annuals, perennials,
tropicals*
Mattituck, New York
landcraftenvironment.com

Living Colors Nursery
bromeliads, orchids
Homestead, Florida
livingcolors.com

Medford Nursery
potted roses, rhododendrons, shrubs
Medford, New Jersey
robertbaker.com

Millane Nurseries
boxwoods, shrubs, trees
Cromwell, Connecticut
millane.com

Moon Nurseries
containerized shrubs, trees
Chesapeake City, Maryland
moonnurseries.com

Murphy John's
annuals, pansies, violas
Sudlersville, Maryland
murphyflower.com

North Creek Nurseries
starter plants and plugs of ferns, ornamental grasses, perennials, shrubs, vines
Oxford, Pennsylvania
northcreeknurseries.com

Otto Keil Florist/ Emma's Garden Growers
annuals, perennials, tropicals
Huntington, New York
ottokeilemmasgarden. blogspot.com

Overdevest Nurseries
perennials, shrubs, trees, vines
Bridgeton, New Jersey
overdevestnurseries.com

Palm Hammock Orchid Estate
rare and exotic plants, aquatics, begonias, orchids, tropicals, vines
Miami, Florida
palmhammockorchidestate.com

Plant Creations
tropicals
Homestead, Florida
plantcreations.com

Plants Delights Nursery
specialty perennials
Raleigh, North Carolina
plantdelights.com

Plantworks Nursery
annuals, grasses, ground covers, hostas
Rougemont, North Carolina
plantworksnursery.com

Pleasant Run Nursery
new plants, unusual woody ornamentals, grasses, perennials, tropicals, vines
Allentown, New Jersey
pleasantrunnursery.com

Prospero Nursery
annuals, conifers, shrubs
White Plains, New York
prosperonursery.com

Richard Lyon's Nursery
fruit trees, heliconia, natives, palms, rare tropicals
Miami, Florida
richardlyonnursery.com

Riggins Nursery
dianthus, hydrangeas, roses, shrubs
Bridgeton, New Jersey
riggins-nursery.com

Rivendell Nursery LLC
shrubs, trees
Greenwich, New Jersey
rivendellnursery.com

Roseland Nursery
potted roses
Acushnet, Massachusetts
roselandroses.com

Schichtel's Nursery
evergreens, fruit trees, shrubs, specimen trees
Springville, New York
schichtels.com

Shade Trees Nursery
container trees, shrubs
Jamesport, New York
shadetreesnursery.com

Sunny Border Nurseries
perennials
Kensington, Connecticut
sunnyborder.com

The Unique Plant
conifers, grasses, Japanese maples, shrubs, trees
Chapel Hill, North Carolina
theuniqueplant.com

Van Engelen
bulbs, peonies
Bantam, Connecticut
vanengelen.com

Waverly Farm
boxwoods, hollies, lilacs, trees, viburnvms
Adamstown, Maryland
waverlyfarm.com

PARTICIPATING FIRMS AND PUBLIC GARDENS

Adam Woodruff + Associates
Clayton, Missouri
adamwoodruff.com

Allworth Design Landscape Architects
Seattle, Washington
allworthdesign.com

Andrea Cochran Landscape Architecture
San Francisco, California
acochran.com

Bernard Trainor + Associates
Monterey, California
bernardtrainor.com

Chanticleer Garden
Wayne, Pennsylvania
chanticleergarden.org

Chicago Park District
Chicago, Illinois
chicagoparkdistrict.com

Colwell Shelor Landscape Architecture
Phoenix, Arizona
colwellshelor.com

deLashmet & Associates
Sagaponack, New York
delashmet.com

Denver Botanic Gardens
Denver, Colorado
botanicgardens.org

Doyle Herman Design Associates
Greenwich, Connecticut and
West Hollywood, California
dhda.com

Elliott Park Campus
Seattle, Washington
elliottparkcampus.com

Elysian Landscapes
Los Angeles, California
elysianlandscapes.com

Greenlee and Associates
Brisbane, California
greenleeandassociates.com

Gustafson Guthrie Nichol
Seattle, Washington
ggnltd.com

HMWhite
New York, New York
hmwhitesa.com

Hoerr Schaudt Landscape Architects
Chicago, Illinois
hoerrschaudt.com

Jeffrey Carbo Landscape Architects
Alexandria, Louisiana
jeffreycarbo.com

Jonathan Alderson Landscape Architects
Wayne, Pennsylvania
jonathanalderson.com

Keith LeBlanc Landscape Architecture
Boston, Massachusetts
kl-la.com

Land Morphology
Seattle, Washington
landmorphology.com

Larry Weaner Landscape Associates
Glenside, Pennsylvania
lweanerassociates.com

Longwood Gardens
Kennett Square, Pennsylvania
longwoodgardens.org

Lutsko Associates
San Francisco, California
lutskoassociates.com

Michael Vergason Landscape Architects
Alexandria, Virginia
vergason.net

Native Prairies Association of Texas
San Marcos, Texas
texasprairie.org

Nelson Byrd Woltz Landscape Architects
Charlottesville, Virginia
nbwla.com

Nievera Williams Design
Palm Beach, Florida
nieverawilliams.com

Northwind Perennial Farm
Burlington, Wisconsin
northwindperennialfarm.com

Oehme, van Sweden
Washington, D.C.
ovsla.com

OLIN Studio
Philadelphia, Pennsylvania and
Los Angeles, California
theolinstudio.com

Raymond Jungles, Inc.
Miami, Florida
raymondjungles.com

Roche+Roche Landscape Architecture
Sonoma, California
rocheandroche.com

Rodney Robinson Landscape Architects
Wilmington, Delaware
rrla.com

Steve Martino Landscape Architect
Phoenix, Arizona
stevemartino.net

Ten Eyck Landscape Architects
Austin, Texas
teneyckla.com

Wolf Landscape Architecture
Westwood, Massachusetts
wolflandscape.com